FAITH AT THE BLACKBOARD

Issues Facing the Christian Teacher

By **BRIAN V. HILL**

WILLIAM B. EERDMANS PUBLISHING COMPANY
GRAND RAPIDS, MICHIGAN

Copyright © 1982 by Wm. B. Eerdmans Publishing Co.
255 Jefferson Ave., SE, Grand Rapids, Mich. 49503
All rights reserved
Printed in the United States of America

Library of Congress Cataloging in Publication Data

Hill, Brian Victor,
  Faith at the blackboard.

  Includes indexes.
  1. Education (Christian theology) I. Title.
BT738.17.H54 1982   371.1'02'0882   82-16377
ISBN 0-8027-1932-X (pbk.)

Contents

Preface

THIS book is an inquiry into the activity of professional teaching from a Christian point of view. It does not assume that the Christian teacher is, or is not, teaching in a Christian school. It does not take sides on the issue of whether there is, or is not, such a thing as Christian education, as distinct from the teaching ministries of evangelism and nurture in the church. But it does assume that when a Christian becomes a professional teacher, he needs to take all that he has been taught about the performance of this role and critique it from the perspective of his Christian beliefs and testimony.

This assessment doesn't automatically happen. The Christian student teacher is tempted to conform obediently and thoughtlessly to the models set before him by his training institution, and later by colleagues in the field. Surely, he says, the experts know best. But no human activity consists entirely of neutral technique. Assumptions about life and the dignity of persons invariably color whatever we do with other people. We may find that the teaching models set before us are built on pagan premises, however plausible their empirical support. The Christian must therefore baptize his professional conduct by interpreting it in the light of biblical insights about the world and human nature.

In the first instance, this kind of examination is conceptual. Because I was trained in graduate school as a philosopher, my preoccupations have been with clarity in our concepts, logic in our arguments, and adequacy in our value-theories and models of thought. Not all the questions to which the Christian educator seeks answers may be resolved by these forms of analysis alone. Many call for more expert biblical and theological exposition;

others require a better knowledge of the actual facts of the case, such as may be obtained by carrying out experimental research and measurement in the field.

Nevertheless, it remains true that until we have conceptualized what we are trying to do in a clear, coherent, and biblical way, we will not know precisely what it is we need to investigate empirically. Hence the kind of inquiry carried out here may prove, I hope, to be a forerunner to many empirical studies and innovative experiments in classrooms and staff rooms, particularly regarding the promotion of Christian values and realism.

Each of the subsequent chapters first appeared in print as a journal article. I acknowledge the permission of the *Journal of Christian Education* to use material on which chapters one, two, four, five, and seven are based. Chapters three and six are based, by permission, on articles published in the journal *Religious Education*. (The specific references for each original article appear on the first page of each chapter.) I am also indebted to many colleagues and audience respondents, but particularly to Dr. Anna Hogg, formerly of Sydney Teachers College, and to Dr. William Andersen of the University of Sydney, who first made me aware of the need to yoke together the personal faith I professed and the vocation of teaching which I was attempting to practice. These two have been models to many others involved in the same task.

I have also been under the tutelage of four young people whose progression from childhood to adolescence has constantly driven me to develop a more concrete theology of the learner and a more interactive approach to learning. To them, and to their wonderful mother, I owe whatever glimpses of love and realism appear in the following pages.

BRIAN HILL

FAITH
AT THE
BLACKBOARD

INTRODUCTION

Thinking Christianly About Teaching

THE young boy who builds a sand castle near the sea's edge dares the lapping waves for two reasons. The first is that wet sand is better for molding and sustaining the shapes of his building. The second is that the waves present a challenge to his skill, assaulting the protective ramparts he is erecting until he proudly closes off the last gap in his defenses, and retreats within to build the interior fortifications and proud towers.

His concentration is admirable. The hours go by, and the detail of his work grows ever finer. But with the passage of the hours comes the turning of the tide, and gradually the waves creep further up the beach and erode the castle walls. Having failed to take tidal energies into account, the boy watches in dismay as his battlements are undermined, his towers topple, and the fine detail is washed away. He turns his back on the ruins and walks home in the gathering darkness.

We may see in this story a parable of a certain conscientious Christian teacher, working cheerfully day by day in the classroom, relatively uninterested in the larger issues surrounding schooling. Originally, he made the decision to become a teacher on the ground that it appeared to offer an opportunity to serve others; he saw great value in interacting with children. He performed his job with great skill and care, and left a mark on many young lives. But his hopes were often frustrated by fellow teachers and school administrators who did not feel dedicated to children in the same way that he did. Curriculum materials that the system pressed upon him often perplexed him and caused him periodic crises of conscience, and mass testing made him angry when it resulted in certain pleasant but slow children being written off as failures. He was similarly perplexed when a strike by militant teachers closed the school for several days, to the detriment of the children's education, and when a campaign conducted at a wider level by a pressure group resulted in what he thought were unwarranted prohibitions placed on what could be taught in the classroom. The teacher watched in dismay as good work was undermined, and wondered what could have been done to prevent it.

The disappointment of such teachers is often so profound that they decide to quit teaching, or at least to quit teaching in the public sector. Why does this happen? There are two possible reasons: one may apply to any teacher, whereas the other applies more specifically to the teacher who also happens to be a committed Christian.

The general reason has to do with the kind of professional training that student teachers receive at many educational institutions. By concentrating on practical teaching skills and methods—the *mechanics* of teaching—it is possible to produce a graduate who can manage a classroom and instruct children with a fair show of efficiency. He will be the kind of teacher who develops predictable routines and instructional sequences into which, each year, he and his pupils will slip smoothly and familiarly. But he will also be the kind of teacher who becomes disturbed when he is asked to leave the beaten path in order to implement new curricula, or to diversify his methods to cater more imaginatively to the differences in the rate and manner of learning among his pupils.

This kind of teacher, the *technician*, looks for the standard techniques which work in the mass, but a *professional person* sees the larger social setting within which his day-to-day activities occur, and has the flexibility to anticipate change, to adapt his methods to new demands, and sometimes to challenge the requirements laid upon him. To produce such professional teachers, training institutions must strike a balance between passing on useful "tricks of the trade" and raising their students' awareness about the meaning of their task within a world and a social order that are changing. These schools must encourage their students to see their daily teaching in the perspective of larger theories of human development and social policy, so that they will not be carried away by every wind of fashion or the craft of salesmen, nor paralyzed by unexpected policy changes and directives.

Christian teachers should be in the forefront of those who seek to constructively criticize training institutions for failing to balance practical preparation with good theory, or vice versa. In the meantime, the individual teacher who senses a lack of critical perspective in his own background should strive for self-improvement through selective reading and, if possible, through reflective discussions with other teachers.

The specifically Christian reason why some teachers lose their zest for teaching is that they have not wrestled to align their educational practice with the values implicit in their Christian commitment. It is obviously Christ-like to care for one's students as persons and to want to help them grow in the right direction. But does this mean that the teacher should be directly evangelistic? A simple affirmation of loving concern will not adequately answer this question. And is it right to submit to the competitive pressures and consumerist priorities of many curricula? Has the teacher any discretion as to what shall be taught in each subject, and how much time is allotted to each?

These and many similar questions should be constantly in the thoughts of teachers who are striving, in their entire lifestyle, not to be conformed to the values and expectations of society at large, but to be transformed by the renewing of their minds through faith in the Lord of all creation. Sadly, many Christian teachers are failing to register an impact for Christ in the general world of education because they have compartmentalized their minds. In one compartment they think about lesson preparation and study the subjects they are teaching; in the other they explore the word of God and grow in worship. But they do not attempt to bring the two together in a way which is both intellectually toughminded and effective in transforming their professional style.

It is my impression that in recent years secular philosophers and humanistic psychologists have had a great effect on public education—so great that many people are questioning its purposes and outcome. Sadly, though a great many teachers are practicing Christians, their impact in the battle of educational ideas is hard to detect. What we have on our hands is a sleeping giant. This is a sad state of affairs, but the process of waking the sleeper can begin at once. We do not have to wait until the number of

Christians in the teaching service reaches a majority, because reforms have always been the work of creative minorities, so committed to their cause that the "silent majority" was eventually
swayed by their bold witness.

The process can begin now, but it must begin with individuals.
Each Christian teacher is thus called to think Christianly about
his or her profession. This book is a contribution to the development of such a way of thinking.

THINKING CHRISTIANLY ABOUT TEACHING

I remember discovering as a beginning teacher that one of my
first challenges was to obtain control in my classes. I had mem-
ories of the teachers of my childhood, who used loud voices,
sarcasm, and the stick to bring their classes to order. Against
these examples I could set the advice given by the teachers in my
training college: to prepare my lessons well, to use motivation,
to appeal to the students' curiosity, and to isolate offenders instead
of punishing the whole group. All would then be well, my in-
structors assured me (exhibiting a beautiful trust in human nature). I also remembered the doctrine of John Dewey, who claimed
that discipline should come from the child's intrinsic interest in
the task, and never from the "because I say so" appeal to authority.

In actual practice, I evolved an effective approach to classroom
control by drawing on both traditional and progressive models
of discipline, and became like the average run of school teachers.
It was some time before I began to ask myself whether my practice was consistent with a Christian view of the nature of persons
and personal relationships. One of the factors that prompted me
to do this was my involvement in a voluntary group for students,
an extra-curricular activity. Relating to them in this informal
group made some of my in-class relationships with those same
youngsters look strained and sub-Christian. I had not *thought
Christianly* about my disciplinary policies, and when I did, I had
to change my way of doing things in the classroom.

We are all tempted to operate with Christian hearts allied to
pagan minds, instead of thinking through all aspects of our living
in order to bring them under Christ's rule. Some years ago, Harry
Blamires identified the need for the development of "the Christian

mind,"[1] but his plea did not have much impact then. More recently, however, his cry has been taken up by writers such as Francis Schaeffer and Os Guinness,[2] and there has been an increase in studies which involve thinking Christianly about many aspects of ordinary living and working. In the more particular sphere of school-teaching as an arena of Christian witness, books and journals have been published that presuppose the teaching of religion in the Christian school, but little writing has specifically addressed itself to the variety of issues facing the Christian who teaches general subjects, particularly in the public school. An exception has been the *Journal of Christian Education*, sponsored over the past twenty years by the Australian Teachers' Christian Fellowship and internationally distributed. Several chapters in this book first appeared in its pages.

The recent authors just mentioned make a very important point about the way in which our thinking is affected by *presuppositions*, basic beliefs which constituted the starting points of any person's thought. The Christian mind is one which has distinctive starting points. It is not enough that we love Christ and think humanistically. We must also *think* as Christ thinks, deriving our presuppositions from his teaching rather than from current philosophical thought and the spirit of the age. This means that we must come to terms with the eternal insights which we believe to be recorded in the Bible. If, for example, something that the Bible says about the nature of persons or the sources of knowledge makes us feel uncomfortable because of our cultural (or professional) conditioning, we must first of all compare Scripture with Scripture to ensure that we are understanding the Bible correctly, and then modify the ideas we have gained from secular philosophy and science in the light of biblical teachings about the nature of reality.

This does not mean that we must throw away all that a non-Christian thinker or scientist says because we cannot accept his initial axioms or general world-view. The reason of the natural man is not totally clouded (nor that of the Christian crystal clear), and we can learn a great deal from God's enemies at those points

---

[1] Harry Blamires, *The Christian Mind* (London: S.P.C.K., 1963).

[2] For example, Francis Schaeffer, *Escape from Reason* (London: InterVarsity Press, 1968); and Os Guinness, *The Dust of Death* (London: InterVarsity Press, 1973).

8   at which they are using God-given reason and imagination in honest and careful inquiry. Conversely, we should not uncritically accept as true all the claims of those thinkers professing to be Christians. Many thinkers put on the Christian label because they admire some of the things that churchmen or the Bible say, at the same time reserving the right to disagree with anything which does not fit into their theory. What they are saying is that that their own reason is their ultimate authority and judge. Yet we are learning from recent philosophy of science that human reason is very vulnerable to ideological bias, that is, the slanting effect of currently fashionable ways of modeling the world. In intellectual terms, the primary meaning of "being a Christian" is being the kind of person who keeps returning to the plain statements of Scripture to assess the ideas and viewpoints that are emerging in his thinking.[3]

Clearly, the Bible does not speak literally and directly to every issue that we encounter. We are to apply its truth to our lives at different levels of generality, depending on how closely the issues come to the personal core of our living. The farther an issue is removed from this center, the greater our need to speculate on the application of biblical principles and their relation to the changing features of contemporary society and technology. The probability that Christians will have varying responses to these issues increases as we move outward, as diagram 1 suggests.

We believe that the main reason God caused the biblical record to come into being, shielding its revelation from inconsistency and error, was to help believers distinguish their private motivations from the facts of the faith. The perspectives of God were mediated through prophets and saintly exemplars until, finally, the communication was completed in the life, teachings, and resurrection of Jesus Christ, and in the commentaries developed on this living Word by the early eye-witness church. Now we know what God is like, we have been given a true account of our human nature, and we have been shown the way to be forgiven and to

---

[3]I say "in intellectual terms" because there are other layers of meaning in the notion of "being a Christian" as well. Christianity is not just an affair of the mind but an inclination of the heart and the will, a constant resolve to affirm Christ's lordship over one's emotions and actions as well as one's cognitions. But the present study focuses on developing a Christian mind as we fulfill our Christian vocation as professional teachers.

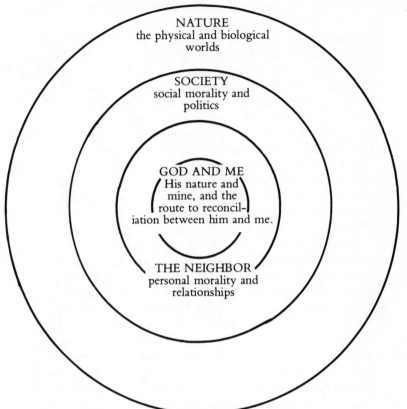

DIAGRAM 1: BIBLICAL TRUTH
AND CONTEMPORARY APPLICATION

become new persons growing progressively more like Christ.

This core of truth is direct and explicit, and allows little spec-
ulation. For example, those liberal Christians in the early decades
of this century who found the teaching about man's basically
sinful disposition too gloomy, or who sought to free theology
from dependence on a real resurrection, were departing from *the
center* of biblical truth, not merely dispensing with non-essentials.
In all honesty they should have relinquished the label of "Christian," for if the Bible is to be respected as the basic documentary

source of our understanding of God and Christianity, then by its own criteria they were preaching a different gospel.

Moving outward from this central core of directly mediated truth, we encounter truths relating to personal relationships and morality. Much of this material consists of examples in the lives of biblical characters, parables and stories that illustrate moral precepts, specific injunctions such as the Ten Commandments and many of Paul's crisp exhortations, and so on. But because the gospel emphasizes liberty, as opposed to legalism, in the Christian life, we have much latitude for personal decision-making after we weigh the factors ourselves. That is, we are provided with *universal principles*—such as the commandment to honor our father and mother—which need to be interpreted and applied in the light of prevailing social customs and lifestyles.

The number of such variables increases greatly as one works outward to the socio-political and natural world. General biblical principles operating at a trans-cultural level have to be worked out in theories of society and natural science which will vary greatly from age to age. The true wonder is that the Bible, originally written in the language and thought-forms of eastern nomads and pastoralists, does provide principles—whether in philosophy, art, or science—which thinkers of all ages have found suggestive and stimulating. But this also means that there will be limitations on the extent to which we will ever be able to claim that we have arrived at *the* Christian view of politics or physical science or art or, in the present case, education—or even *the* one true Christian theory in any one of these areas *for our time*. For the same broad principles may validate a number of different sets of policy and practice, and permit a range of theories seeking to explain the same group of phenomena.

Our best course of action is to identify particular Christian principles and values which have an obvious bearing on the area of our concern, and to put them to work in that area. This is what I have attempted to do in this book. I have identified a number of questions which concern, or should concern, Christian teachers, and have discussed each one in the light of relevant biblical principles and current educational theory. I am open to attack on either flank! But more important than whether you agree with the particular things I say is whether you will find this book helpful in your efforts to become the sort of teacher who

tends to think Christianly about his or her work life, and to
witness in the profession.

A FRAMEWORK FOR INQUIRY

If we wish to develop a Christian social consciousness about
teaching, where shall we begin? Teaching is a highly complex
activity involving numerous variables. Here is one way of identifying topics of concern.

We may begin by seeing teaching as a situation in which the
teacher is trying to help the student to come to terms with his
world. That gives us what may be called "a triangle of forces,"
as sketched in diagram 2.

Concentrating on *the student*, we find it necessary to view him
in two different ways: (1) as an organism with certain developmental potentials, to be understood psychologically, and (2) as
a person with dignity, rights, and purposes. The first of these
raises questions about how we understand individual development, and whether there are available Christian critiques of the
psychological models presented to us in our training. (There are!)
The second view raises questions about the freedom of the child.
Can we, for example, use compulsion in education? Both concepts draw on biblical insights about the nature of children and
of people in society.

Out of these considerations emerge educational objectives for
helping students develop into mature persons—objectives that
relate to nurturing in them certain ways of knowing and feeling,

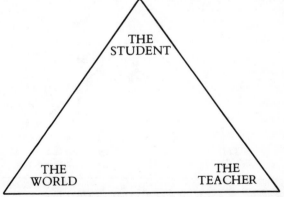

DIAGRAM 2: THE TRIANGLE OF FORCES IN TEACHING

DIAGRAM 3: THE STUDENT

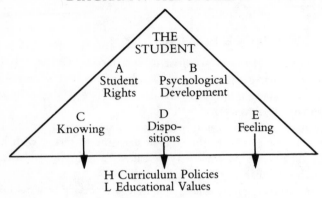

and the encouragement of desirable mental and moral dispositions. All of this can be put in summary form, as it is in diagram 3.

Next, looking at *the world* to which we are introducing the
student, we find the more organized and objective aspects of
learning, represented by bodies of knowledge. Most institutions
of formal education pay close attention to "subject matter" and
the transmission of facts about things, ideas, and people. The
Bible has much to say about all three, and Christian critique of
current theories of knowledge is not lacking. But the world also
has more elusive and subjective aspects, relating to cultural change
and social problems, which need to be studied within individual
situations and with a sense of involvement. These may be represented as they are in diagram 4.

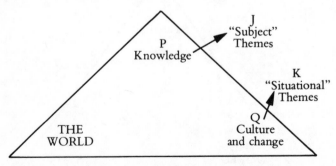

DIAGRAM 4: THE WORLD

In bringing the two together, *the teacher* has a professional concern to develop effective strategies of teaching and testing, bearing in mind at the same time that the nature of his relationships with his pupils not only facilitates formal learning but is in itself a curriculum of educative experiences. The personal factor also enters into the way in which the teacher sees himself in relation to other people, in particular to professional colleagues. These considerations yield diagram 5.

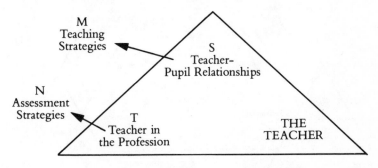

DIAGRAM 5: THE TEACHER

When all three expanded headings are put back into our original triangle of forces, three additional topics also need to be accommodated. The first relates to *further education and training*, because Christian theorists have tended to neglect questions of education for later life: work, leisure, and re-training. The second focuses on *special educational needs* such as the needs of learners who are in some way handicapped or disadvantaged to a degree which prejudices their achievement in conventional school settings. (I include here the problems of ethnic and religious minorities in societies with aggressive dominant cultures.) The third set of issues relates to *community support structures* and parental involvement. It also raises questions about the relative importance we attach to educational experiences other than those provided by the school, such as those provided by the home, the voluntary group, and the media. Amalgamating all these concerns, we get diagram 6.

Here, then, is a substantial agenda for the thinking Christian to tackle in the effort to apply the Christian gospel to the profes-

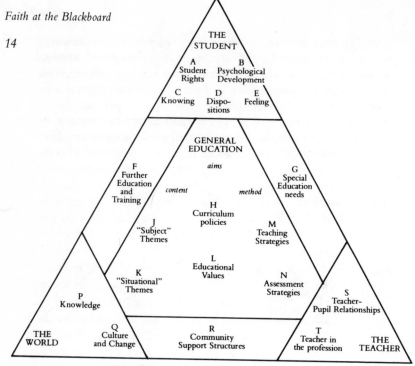

DIAGRAM 6: THE TRIANGLE OF
FORCES IN TEACHING (EXPANDED)

sion and structures of education. Although this book cannot cover
more than a fraction of the ground, the sample of topics chosen
may usefully typify the kind of job to be done.

SYNOPSIS: THE SAMPLE

Assuming that any topic chosen will tend to apply in some way
to the center of the diagram—that is, in relation to the aims,
content, and method of teaching—how effectively do the questions asked in the subsequent chapters of this book sample the
areas surrounding this core?

Chapter One asks, "Should I be in favor of compulsion in
education?" Most teachers take for granted that there are schools
to which all children must go for a part of their lives, and subjects
which they must study. The reflective teacher, however, must
inquire whether this mentality of compulsion is desirable. Does

it help children to learn, or does it stunt their desire and curiosity? The Christian teacher must face up to the question of whether there are some respects in which children need to be compelled to do things for their own alleged good. Thus, our central concern here is with *A: Student Rights*.

Chapter Two asks, "Should I put relationships or subject matter first in my teaching?" In current educational literature there is a vigorous controversy about the relative educational priority to be given to interpersonal relationships in the classroom over against systematic instruction in the standard "subjects." Humanistic psychologists argue on both sides of this debate. Where does the Christian teacher stand? This topic oscillates between the themes *C: Knowing* and *E: Feeling*, and between *P: Knowledge* and *S: Teacher-Pupil Relationships*.

Chapter Three asks, "Is it possible and desirable to teach religion in schools?" Countries vary greatly in their ideas about what kind of religious instruction, if any, should be allowed in public schools. Christian teachers are often consulted on the assumption that they will naturally have an informed professional view of the matter. In fact, however, many are quite equivocal about it, finding their desire to spread the Christian faith at odds with their perception of the purposes of general education. Are we to aim at imparting knowledge (*C: Knowing*) or promoting commitment (*D: Dispositions*)? Such questions are central not merely to the teaching of religion but to *L: Educational Values* in general.

Chapter Four asks, "Should I really be teaching in a Christian school?" Over the centuries, the Christian churches have been very active in general education. Does the Bible lay down as the ideal that *all* a child's formal education must be provided by Christians? Do recent cultural changes (*Q: Culture and Change*) oblige us to rethink the nature of Christian involvement? Is it possible for a Christian teaching in a public school (*T: Teacher in the Profession*) to be where God wants him to be?

Chapter Five asks, "Should I promote community involvement in my school?" Some teachers resent and fear parental pressure; others welcome it. What is a Christian view of the relationship between home and school (*R: Community Support Structures*)?

Chapter Six asks, "Dare I let my students know where I stand

16   personally as a Christian?" Teachers are strongly pressured to be neutral guides of the young, concealing their own beliefs and values for fear of exercising undue influence over other people's children. Can the Christian teacher be content with this role? How far ought he to go in influencing his pupils? This topic bears particularly on *A: Student Rights* and *S: Teacher-Pupil Relationships*.

Chapter Seven asks, "What should my style be as a professional teacher?" Some teachers enjoy exercising authority over students; others like to appear to be knowledge experts; still others want to be friendly counselors who let the student decide what he should learn. What view should the Christian teacher take of her role in relation to students and staff? Both *S: Teacher-Pupil Relations* and *T: Teacher in the Profession* are at stake in the asking of this question.

Two things may be said about this sample. First, it samples most of the themes mentioned in the diagram—but, second, sampling is all it does. Each heading suggests a range of issues which have not been touched on here. For example, though we appear to have dealt with *T: Teacher in the Profession* in at least two of our topics, a moment's thought will reveal that there are many other aspects still to be explored under this heading. Some that occurred to me include personal development, the mental health of teachers, apologetics in the staff room, further in-service studies, research interests, responses to innovation, promotion, the teacher as a public servant, working conditions, teacher induction, teacher power, unions and teachers, and the clerically ordained principal.

These topics indicate the great scope for future dialogue among teachers who want to think Christianly about their professional task and witness. I hope that *Faith at the Blackboard* will invite both criticism and improved imitation.

1 Compulsory Education

"Should I be in favor of compulsory strategies in education?"

IN the minds of most people, the notions of "compulsion" and "education" tend to go together. They seem to have much territory in common: there has never been a time when someone was not requiring someone else to suffer instruction "for his own good." Even parents—perhaps because they themselves rely on compulsion quite often—have generally accepted without question the school's right to impose sanctions, though they also seem to think, sometimes, that their own children deserve to be exempt from them.

This chapter asks what justifications, if any, support the use of compulsory strategies in education. Some people may think that compulsion in education is so obviously a dismal fact of life that we could better spend our time seeking grounds for increasing freedom in education. I, too, am adamant in my desire to liberate children from the coercive monotony into which so much of our schooling has lapsed. We should welcome any efforts to bring about this freedom, and we as Christians should be alert to the questions being raised (by people such as Ivan Illich and John Holt) about the ethics of much that goes on in traditional schools, regardless of the fact that such questions do not always come from the pens of Christians.[1]

An earlier version of this chapter appeared as "Compulsion and Education," Journal of Christian Education, *Papers 52, Aug. 1975, pp. 39-57.*

[1]Ivan Illich's *Deschooling Society* (New York: Harper & Row, 1970) is well known, as are the books by John Holt, beginning with *How Children Fail* (New York: Penguin Books, 1965). Since A. S. Neill's famous school is often sentimentalized by modern advocates of the free school, it is useful to know about the collection of essays, some supportive and some critical, entitled *Summerhill: For and Against* (Sydney, Australia: Angus & Robertson, 1972). Other relevant studies will be referred to in more detail later on in this chapter.

But it is one thing to extend the areas of freedom in education for good moral and educational reasons; it is quite another to lose one's nerve as an educational administrator and to surrender responsibility to active pressure groups because one has no thought-out position regarding the exercise of one's own authority. It is even more alarming if some of those same pressure groups are seeking influence in the schools either to restrict children's educational options for over-paternalistic reasons (as some Christians would like to do), or, in the name of openness, to promote a naive view of man or a political revolution (as some neo-Marxists advocate[2]).

I have therefore chosen—somewhat perversely, perhaps—to look for justifications of compulsion in education, hoping thereby to provoke others to come up with more rational proposals for greater freedom in education. This strategy may have another useful outcome as well: showing where compulsion *is* needed in education may also imply where it *is not* desirable, and thereby increase the possibilities for freedom.

I also want to show that what is at stake is not just conceptual clarity about what we are doing, nor merely different empirical claims about what actual effects various forms of compulsion have on learners, but ethical values. The crucial issues involve beliefs about human nature and society, and about the way in which we should treat persons-in-the-making—precisely what makes the topic so relevant to the Christian thinker. Such questions of value and the nature and destiny of persons are not solely in the jurisdiction of experts such as psychologists and teachers. Indeed, in this sense there are no experts; it is for the community to arrive at a consensus of what it expects of the schools. In such a dialogue, especially as it touches on compulsion and freedom to learn, there is great potential for Christians to be a positive and leavening influence.

SHARPENING THE ISSUES

Contrasting the arguments of two books published in 1973 brings out the points at issue. In *Must We Educate?* Carl Bereiter argues

[2]See, for example, Paulo Freire, *Pedagogy of the Oppressed*, trans. Myra Bergman Ramos (London: Herder and Herder, 1970); and the less honest *Teaching as a Subversive Activity* by Neil Postman and Charles Weingartner (New York: Delacorte, 1969)—less honest because in fact the authors play to the gallery with their title and are more authoritarian than they pretend.

that we have no right to do more than inculcate very basic skills—roughly, the "three R's of the elementary school."[3] All other content, he believes, is an invasion of personality, unless the learner has freely elected to study it. Thus, in the name of a "philosophy of freedom," Bereiter denies the legitimacy of any educational purposes which, however idealistic, determine what kind of person the student will probably become, an approach that accounts for his dislike of the term "educate." "The only kind of teaching that is truly non-authoritarian," he says, "is skill training, for competence in general gives the individual more power and freedom of choice."[4]

The second book, entitled *Towards a Compulsory Curriculum*, is by John White.[5] He is alarmed at the extent to which British schools have departed from the notion that children should take a basic minimum of required studies. Writing in the carefully analytic style of an English philosopher, White argues that several areas of study are necessary to the education of each child, an argument that produces a fairly traditional list weighted toward the academic disciplines. This is not to say that White is unaware of the ethical problem raised by Bereiter, and by many greater men before him. He recognizes that he has to provide adequate reasons for infringing on whatever freedom the beginning learner possesses, and he makes an interesting attempt to do so (something I shall draw on later in this chapter).

Somewhere between the poles represented by these two books lies the solution to our inquiry. It is not possible to short-circuit the discussion by seizing on some conveniently dogmatic religious teaching, such as the verse in Proverbs which counsels parents to exercise strong correction.[6] For the Scriptures not only advocate consistently that children be given clear admonition concerning the moral law, but also stress the dignity of each individual in God's eyes, epitomized by the individual's right and

[3]Carl Bereiter, *Must We Educate?* (Englewood Cliffs, N.J.: Prentice-Hall, 1975), p. 35.

[4]Bereiter, p. 8. Insisting that a philosophy of freedom includes even the right not to learn, Bereiter makes possible the abandonment of children who don't know what is best for themselves.

[5]John P. White, *Towards A Compulsory Curriculum* (London: Routledge & Kegan Paul, 1973).

[6]Proverbs 13:24. Unless otherwise indicated, all biblical citations are from the New International Version.

capacity to make choices for himself, even regarding acceptance of God's rule. Today there is the potential for divergent views even among thinkers who draw many of their presuppositions from the Bible and Christian tradition, exemplified in the Roman Catholic fold by the radical critiques of Ivan Illich and Paulo Freire on the one hand, and the confident prescriptions of Jacques Maritain on the other.[7] If anything, Evangelicals hold even more diverse views.

THE LOGIC OF FREEDOM

The heart of the problem lies in the issue of whether it is ever *morally* legitimate for one person to exercise power over another person. A particularization of this question is whether teachers have the right to exercise power over learners. Most current writers on the subject look back to Mill's essay "On Liberty"[8] for the classic formulation of this problem, and Mill does indeed outline the case clearly, though he was not the first to do so. One should also note that Mill was dependent on assumptions about the nature of man and society which are more profound than his principle of utility allows for.

Mill insists that each individual has the right to pursue his own interests in his own way, so long as he does not interfere with anyone else's pursuit of his interests. This "keep off each other's patch" concept of liberty allows A to exercise compulsion over B only if B trespasses on A's patch.[9] This is a very individualistic and rather negative view of freedom, though Mill does restrict it to the situation in an allegedly civilized society.

He then allows for exceptions to this rule in the case of those who are immature: on the domestic level, children, and on the international level, barbarians. This gives rise to a second concept of liberty, which permits A to intervene in the affairs of B if it helps B to develop into a mature person, capable of free and equal

---

[7]Thus Illich, *Deschooling Society*, Freire, *Pedagogy of the Oppressed*, and Jacques Maritain, *The Education of Man*, ed. Donald and Idella Gallagher (New York: Doubleday, 1962).

[8]John Stuart Mill, *Utilitarianism; On Liberty; Representative Government* (London: J. M. Dent, 1954), pp. 65-170.

[9]Cf. Mill, pp. 72-73.

discussion.[10] Actually, this second concept can be made to nullify the first, expecially if one chooses to argue that one's neighbor, though adult, is immature, and therefore one is justified in trespassing on his patch. But Mill at least provides the safeguard that, even then, the trespass must be made in the neighbor's interest, and the burden of proof is on the trespasser (teacher? welfare worker? policeman? parson?) to show that this is the case.

It is important to remember what Mill takes for granted in his presentation of the issue. Notable is his assumption that, although many human beings are incompetent, at least some of them are mature and so capable of free thought and action. As we shall see later, this assumption has been seriously disputed, and needs underpinnings. Secondly, Mill assumes that if B sees that A is capable of free thought and action, then B will naturally accord to A the right to free thought and action. But this idea, too, requires underpinnings. Respect for other persons does not come easily, even to the most rational of men, and even in situations in which it appears to have the most practical utility.[11]

How does the logic of freedom bear on education? It is clear that teachers, like a number of other agents including parents, policemen, and physicians, do on occasion infringe on the liberties of certain individuals. And the compulsion they exercise need not necessarily be obvious or distasteful. Even Bereiter recognizes that when educational progressivists claim that they are leaving the child free to learn as he chooses, they are merely disguising the fact that they have structured the learning environment with certain goals in view, goals to which the child has not been, and cannot yet be, a party.[12] Thus it seems that the educator, admitting that his activities infringe on the individual's liberty, has one of two choices: to produce plausible overriding reasons for continuing to intervene in the learner's life, or to throw in the towel and leave the learner free to learn or not to learn at his own discretion.

---

[10]F. J. Crittenden has a neat gloss on this point in "Education and Society: A Critique of Ivan Illich's *Deschooling Society*," in *Concepts in Education*, ed. J. V. D'Cruz and P. J. Sheehan (Melbourne, Australia: Dove Publications, 1974), p. 80.

[11]I have argued the importance of presuppositional underpinnings for this notion in my book *Education and the Endangered Individual* (New York: Teachers College Press, 1973).

[12]Bereiter, *Must We Educate?*, pp. 31f.

Recent radical literature contains many examples of theorists who embrace the second alternative, notably Ivan Illich. Suspicious as he is that the very notion of "teacher" connotes pupil dependency, Illich prefers to speak of "skill models" whom the voluntary learner is free to consult. Likewise, he rejects the idea of "school" because it reeks of "the axiom that learning is the result of teaching."[13] Though I find Illich's writing bracing and his criticisms of the consumer society penetrating, I cannot accept his idealized image of man and society, both for Christian reasons and other reasons. In particular, the situation of his idealized learner is far removed from the real-life situation of the average *child*.

Since I decline to accept the second alternative and abdicate the educator's role, I must embrace the first alternative and defend this role, first by taking issue with the logic of freedom as expounded by Mill. While his account establishes a presumption in favor of letting people do what they want, it does recognize that there can be grounds for interfering with the activities of others. Here, unfortunately, is a loophole for heavy paternalism and rationalized tyranny which Mill neglected to guard against, and which I would argue can only be closed off by a view of the nature and worth of the individual higher than the one Mill possessed.

AUTONOMOUS BEING OR AUTOMATON?

One view which has a very wide following in educational psychology is the radical behaviorism of B. F. Skinner. He emphatically rejects the notion of a free or autonomous man, insisting that human persons are whatever their conditioning makes them. It is his hope that behavioral science will produce people conditioned to be happy and creative. Aware of C. S. Lewis's argument that scientists who do not respect the dignity of man are abolishing man, Skinner frankly concedes the point without a qualm by remarking that "what is being abolished is autonomous man. . . . His abolition has been long overdue."[14] This is naive

[13]Illich, *Deschooling Society*, p. 28.
[14]B. F. Skinner, *Beyond Freedom and Dignity* (New York: Alfred A. Knopf, 1971), p. 200. See also C. S. Lewis, *The Abolition of Man* (London: Geoffrey Bles, 1947), esp. pp. 39-48; and Brian V. Hill, "Behavior, Learning and Control: Some Philosophical Difficulties in the Writings of B. F. Skinner," *Educational Theory*, 22 (Spring 1972), 230-241.

scientific determinism at its most brash, reflected in the addiction of some educators to scientifically prescribed curricula, behavioral objectives, teaching machines, programmed instruction, and candy bribes to reinforce learning—tactics which exclude other useful modes of teaching and learning that do not fit the behaviorist's model.

In reaction to presumptuous scientism of this type, existentialist writers, including many Christian thinkers, have hammered home the view that, if freedom is an illusion, it is nevertheless the strongest illusion we have, and for practical purposes at least it must function as the truth we live by. We are choosing beings: we experience choices and live *in* them. Christian existentialists, of course, make the point more strongly by embedding this truth not in subjective awareness but in the teaching that this is an attribute of God's image in man.

Now this dictum can be developed into the extreme view that every moment the self begins again, free to forsake its past choices, as atheistic existentialists tend to claim. This is absurd. If it is admitted that our choices can modify the future, then our past history must be a record of the modifications brought about in us by our previous choices, and by the choices of others. The natural environment also limits the scope of our choices. A freedom which ignores these constraints of the physical world and what Niebuhr calls "the dramas of history"[15] is no freedom at all, but a state no better than that of a lost child.

Common sense, which is enshrined in personal relationships, the arts, and the practices of the law courts, presupposes a capacity for freedom which may be increased or constricted by circumstances. I sense that ordinary people look for underpinnings of this belief, only to find that the social sciences give them cold comfort because they are predicated on deterministic models. The justification I find most persuasive is found at the religious level: the Christian faith offers the reasonable belief that man's nature is such that it enables him to share the conscious life of God. It says his highest enjoyment is to choose to serve God, and admonishes him to grow in the knowledge of God—that is, to

[15]Reinhold Niebuhr, *The Self and the Dramas of History* (London: Faber & Faber, 1955), pp. 56f.

24   develop and enlarge his powers of thought, feeling, and choice in ways consistent with God's will.[16]

Many people may not be prepared to accept all that these beliefs imply. But we can expect to share much common ground in dialogue with the average parent and citizen on the conditions necessary for children to attain greater personal freedom and self-understanding.

THE KNOWLEDGE CONDITION

One area of agreement would be the conviction that freedom begins, in Marx's words, with the recognition of necessity—that is, with an understanding of the laws that govern our physical social, and spiritual being. "The truth," as Jesus said, "will set you free" (John 8:32).

In this sense, the more we know about the discoveries, achievements, and modes of perception which we as modern persons are heir to, the freer we are to get the most out of our experiences and to rise above our cultural conditioning. It is both ironic and significant that the most telling criticisms of our Western educational systems are coming from some of the most highly qualified "products" of those systems.

All this amounts to the assertion that freedom has a knowledge condition, "knowledge" in this phrase meaning an understanding of, and empathy with, all the public realms of meaning which bear on human thought and action. It may not be easy to arrive at the truth in these realms, and in many cases we may have to be content with successively better approximations of it, but at least we believe that it is there to be discovered. And its discovery progressively enlarges our options.

Such arguments must have considerable appeal to the Christian, for the Bible constantly stresses the need to *know* what is good and true, and to choose knowingly for oneself which way to go.[17] Paternalistic pastors and schoolteachers have from time

[16]See, for example, Genesis 1:26; Psalm 8:3-6; Psalm 119:33-48; and Romans 6:15-19.

[17]On understanding the choices one makes, see, for example, Deuteronomy 4:1-9; Psalm 39:4-6; Proverbs 25:2; Jeremiah 9:23-24; and Mark 12:33; Romans 2:11-16; 1 Corinthians 14:14-16; Hebrews 8:10-12. On being responsible for one's choices, see, for example, Deuteronomy 28:1 and 15; Joshua 24:14-15; I Kings 18:21; Ezekiel 3:16-21; and Matthew 7:21-29; Acts 5:1-6; Romans 8:12-13; James 1:22-25.

to time preferred to keep their flock ignorant of the options they considered bad for them, leaving them placidly locked into customary styles of life and pious observance; but judged by biblical rule, these policies have been sub-Christian and have dishonored God.

THE DEVELOPMENTAL CONDITION

The second requirement for the exercise of human freedom may be called a developmental condition, something Mill recognized in his reference to "maturity." This development involves more than just growing up in the automatic sense often indicated by the term "maturation": it includes both acculturation and the achievement of a critical awareness of one's cultural milieu. Without the help of parents and other supportive adults, most children would not even survive, because they do not initially grasp what is in their best interests, especially in a culture which has grown so complex that it has transformed the simplest animal functions into intricate and technology-dependent rituals. Yet without the development of a critical consciousness, they would remain contented slaves; hence the knowledge condition.

It is unlikely that many would disagree with what I have just said, although some educators talk so glibly about leaving children free to learn whatever they choose that they appear to ignore the developmental condition. The question most often debated is whether adult guides function wholly as facilitators, providing resources when the child voluntarily seeks them, and trusting the child's innate drives and intelligence to turn him in the direction he needs to go; or whether it is necessary in the child's interest to compel him to go in certain directions.

There are two questions here, one ethical and one empirical. The ethical question is, have we the *right* to dictate our values and preferences to the child by compelling him to perform certain learning tasks? The empirical question is, *can* compulsion lead the child into freedom? It is interesting to see how these two questions interact in the literature of what is being called "open education."

Terms like "open education" and "free schools" have become slogans for a number of projects to reform education, and many references have been made to the "informal" primary schools described in the British Plowden Report. One often gets the impression that all compulsory elements have been purged from such schools through the adoption of open-classroom, integrated-day activities. Yet attendance is compulsory, and, as one perceptive American observer notes, the teacher usually exerts great control over the kind of environment she creates to house the informal activities of learning, because her aim is to equip the child with the same understanding and skills that the best formal schools also seek to develop in their students.[18]

In other words, such schools make empirical claims to be leading the child toward personal autonomy more effectively than more formally structured schools, but they are not usually questioning the propriety of working toward that particular vision of an educated person. An interesting illustration of this point is found in the critique which R. S. Peters and some of his associates wrote on the Plowden Report. For the most part the argument is about *means*, because both sides basically agree on the goal of personal autonomy, and are far from questioning the teacher's right to lead children toward it in the ways they advocate.[19]

But certain other exponents of open education go much farther than those criticized by Peters. They decline to enter the debate over whether open or closed-classroom procedures are the *best* means to adopt, because they have already decided that, in ethical terms, open procedures are the *only* means. They are convinced that all else is an invasion of personal freedom. One writer goes so far as to refer to the very act of creating an educational situation as an "original sin"—though it is, she concedes, one from which we cannot escape![20]

Exponents of this kind of openness, such as Illich and Carl Rogers,[21] seem to see all learners as instant adults with innately good natural impulses to learn the right things and to apply the necessary self-discipline. Many of them are also unwilling to come

[18]Theodore Manolakes, "Introduction: The Open Education Movement," *The National Elementary Principal*, 52 (Nov. 1972), 44. On the diversity of viewpoints concealed by the fashionable slogan of "open education," see Brian V. Hill, "What's 'Open' about Open Education?" in *Philosophy of Open Education*, ed. David Nyberg (London: Routledge & Kegan Paul, 1975), pp. 3-13.

[19]See R. S. Peters, ed., *Perspectives on Plowden* (London: Routledge & Kegan Paul, 1969).

[20]Hazel Barnes, *An Existentialist Ethics* (New York: Alfred A. Knopf, 1967), p. 290.

[21]Illich, *Deschooling Society*, and Carl R. Rogers, *Freedom to Learn* (New York: Charles E. Merrill, 1969), e.g., pp. 152 and 282.

to grips with the sophisticated forms of life that technological civilization demands of us. For example, many counter-cultural proposals exhibit a strong nostalgia for the "simple life" of the pre-industrial village. I find such views of openness distinctly implausible, and neglectful of both the developmental condition mentioned here and the spiritual condition I shall discuss next.

Justifying compulsion as a legitimate or ethical strategy in the education of developing persons would be much easier if we possessed empirical proof that it could lead to greater freedom of thought and action in the mature or developed individual. Current debates on this issue involve much assertion and counter-assertion: radicals claim that the "products" of compulsory education are all shackled by value commitments they have no hope of reviewing critically, while mainline theorists make opposite claims.

There are, however, straws in the wind. Andersen cites psychological evidence that smaller children need the protection of a fairly authoritative environment to stabilize the development of a "self" before they can embark on self-criticism and the examination of alternative values.[22] R. S. Peters and others have linked the goal of autonomy with the development of reason, and appeal to the work of Piaget and Kohlberg for empirical support.[23] Nevertheless, much research of a difficult longitudinal kind still needs to be done to show whether particular compulsory strategies improve or impede the emergence of rational autonomy. In the meantime, the *prima facie* case for some sort of compulsion is amusingly illustrated by a quotation from an article by Ralph M. Miller, although it oversimplifies the complex problem of justifying particular kinds of educational intervention:

[22]W. E. Andersen, "Ideological Education," Diss. University of Sydney 1965, pp. 60-98.

[23]For example, R. S. Peters, "Education and Human Development" in *Melbourne Studies in Education*, 1969, ed. R. J. W. Selleck (Melbourne, Australia: Melbourne University Press, 1970), pp. 83-103. It is important to note that Kohlberg, even though he professes to be guided by empirical data and therefore to be developing a "natural" account of the mature individual, admits to a philosophical commitment to such champions of rational autonomy as Kant and Hare in deciding on his experimental model. See Lawrence Kohlberg, "Stages of Moral Development as a Basis for Moral Education," in *Moral Education: Interdisciplinary Approaches*, ed. C. M. Beck et al. (Toronto: University of Toronto Press, 1971), pp. 43, 46, 55, 69.

The child, or even the naive tourist, who chooses to hand-feed the bears, may not thank us for leaving him free to make that choice if it results in his being mauled. It is a choice he would not have made had he known better. . . . [It] is a paltry freedom which merely removes restraints, or even provides opportunities without providing the basis of knowledge which enables discriminating choice among possibilities.[24]

THE SPIRITUAL CONDITION

I come now to the third and most difficult condition I associate with the idea of freedom of thought and action: the spiritual situation of man as a fallen creature. The apostle Paul summed up this condition when he said, "So then, I myself in my mind am a slave to God's law, but in the sinful nature a slave to the law of sin."[25] What Paul is saying is that the most mature of persons is still involved in an internal civil war between what he rationally believes to be good and a perverse inclination to do what is wrong. On some occasions he may even know that what he chooses is not in his own best interest, but he makes the choice simply because it is autonomous—a rebel gesture against God or morality or society or whatever he sees as authority.

Paul's saying is a hard one. Attempts have been made to blame deliberate wrongdoing on immaturity, ignorance, social disadvantage, and mental weakness, but they all founder on the rock of what Kierkegaard calls "defiant will."[26] Moreover, the sense of guilt generated by sin is not to be shrugged off as mere "guilt feelings," a pathological state in some people.[27] Sometimes we feel guilty because we *are* guilty—by our own code, whatever that may be and however rational our adoption of it. At other times we do not feel guilty, but we should; our conduct has blatantly flouted the principles we profess and enjoin others to follow. Selfishness and callousness, for example, particularly in

---

[24]Ralph M. Miller, "Responsibility for Freedom," *The Journal of Educational Thought*, 7 (Dec. 1973), 147.

[25]Romans 7:25. See also Philippians 1:6; James 3:1-2; I John 1:8-10; etc.

[26]Sören Kierkegaard, *The Sickness Unto Death*, trans. Walter Lowrie (Princeton, N.J.: Princeton University Press, 1941), p. 145.

[27]See Martin Buber's interesting essay on "Guilt and Guilt Feelings" in *The Knowledge of Man*, ed. Maurice Friedman, trans. Maurice Friedman and Ronald Gregor Smith (London: George Allen & Unwin, 1965), pp. 123-148.

the best-educated nations, have more to do with the crises beset-
ting today's world than commentators usually care to admit.

For reasons such as these I mistrust "personal autonomy" as
the declared primary goal of human development, and am leery
of unbridled free expression as the means. I am not confident that
urging people to "do their own thing," to be "authentic," or to
affirm their own existence will result in the best state of affairs
for society, or even for the persons concerned. Autonomy does
no more than bring us to the starting line of personal choice.
How we run thereafter depends on our spiritual adjustment even
more than on our degree of maturity or rationality.

All this leads up to the Christian claim that all men stand in
need of spiritual readjustment, which is triggered by a conscious
resolve to submit to the living God, supremely revealed to us in
the Christ of the Christian Scriptures. This is not to claim that
such a resolve brings instant freedom from perverse inclination.
But the Bible implies that a new developmental process com-
mences in which the harmony between inclination and obligation
becomes more and more firmly established—the biblical word
for it is "peace"—thus freeing the personality to make choices
that are more loving and creative.[28]

How do these claims of Christian belief about our spiritual
condition relate to the issue of freedom versus compulsion in
education? And are our conclusions in any way accessible to the
non-believer? These are enormously complicated issues which
need much more attention from modern Christian theorists, and
here it is only possible to make three suggestions.

First, if the phenomenon of deliberate perversity in choosing
does exist, then any human community—including the school—
must at times restrain its members from folly and wrongdoing
when it cannot persuade them to restrain themselves. Of course,
when there is considerable disagreement about what constitutes
wrongdoing, social regulation must be confined to the areas of
general agreement, and these are difficult to obtain. But it is no
solution to the difficulty to dispense with laws and regulations,
or to deny to constituted authorities, like magistrates and prin-
cipals, the power to administer them. We fence off railway lines

[28]The perfectionism espoused by some sects is clearly denied by the biblical
writers, e.g., Romans 6:12-14; 7:5-13; Galatians 6:1-4; Hebrews 4:14-16; I John
1:5-2:2.

because perverse adults, as well as children, could hurt themselves by walking on the tracks. We forbid drug trafficking and make drug education compulsory because wicked men exploit fools, whether ignorant or perverse or both. Laws and rules restrict individual freedom, but they are the lesser evil in those instances in which their absence would threaten it even more. One does not have to accept the claims of Christian belief to assent to this proposition, which even John Stuart Mill can espouse, though I believe that the Christian explanation of why the world is in this state makes the most sense.

Second, if perverse inclination is not confined to the ignorant, but overtakes mature adults and even, at times, those who are becoming spiritually adjusted, then no perfect state of affairs is possible, and we must be content with the most satisfactory expedients. This puts a different slant on the question why, and how far, we should support democracy. Some theorists have seen in the vision of democracy, whether liberal or socialist, the prospect of utopia in human affairs. And utopian visions are still with us; take, for example, the writings of Illich. Much truer to the biblical viewpoint, however, is Reinhold Niebuhr's famous aphorism: "Man's capacity for justice makes democracy possible; but his inclination to injustice makes democracy necessary."[29] There is a blend of idealism and realism in this remark which is much-needed in policies of school administration and curriculum selection, a subject I will discuss later in more detail. Here it is sufficient to say that while democratically based decision-making may be tedious and inefficient, it is generally safer than autocracy or bureaucracy. Even so, the Christian also recognizes, and on the same grounds, that there may come a point at which a democratically made decision must be opposed on higher grounds of objective morality. In a sinful world there is no guarantee that men may not make morally depraved agreements about what lifestyles are to be encouraged or permitted in their community.

Third, if the good life is impossible without spiritual readjustment, then education must either include the objective of religious conversion or confine itself to a more limited objective. Some advocates of open education talk as though it will be the salvation

---

[29]Quoted by John C. Bennett in "Reinhold Niebuhr's Social Ethics" in *Reinhold Niebuhr: His Religious, Social and Political Thought*, ed. Charles W. Kegley and Robert W. Bretall (New York: Macmillan, 1961), p. 50.

of the race, foreshadowing a society of free, liberated persons—
an apocalyptic society its supporters sometimes describe in Marxist terms. They have taken over the role of theorists of an earlier
day who looked to the schools to achieve religious commitment,
racial integration, social conformity, and a host of other life-sized
objectives. I think the wiser course is to regard education as an
important resource within the greater project of salvation, guid-
ing the immature and the uninformed toward enlightenment about
their present condition, and the options that are open to them.
This suggests that the goal of autonomy, though not adequate to
the project of living, is probably appropriate to the process of
formal education, especially where compulsion is involved. At
any rate, current analysis of the concepts of education in ordinary
language[30] suggests that one could hope for wide consensus among
parents and teachers that formal education should be regarded in
this way.

DIGRESSION: THE VOLUNTARY MOTIF

At this point it is appropriate to digress for a moment to consider
the question of what needs to be said about *voluntary* strategies
in education in order to balance the main thrust of this chapter.
First, it is important to emphasize that the three conditions of
freedom spelled out above are all matters of degree. Except perhaps in the very earliest stages of growth, the learner is not without some knowledge on which to base his choices, however limited
and highly specific that knowledge may be. The promise of education is that it will increase his options. *Second*, development
is gradual, not sudden, and there is no point at which we can say,
now the learner has begun to choose autonomously. Small children have many autonomous moments. *Third*, spiritual perversity is a tendency, not an inevitability, and many choices at all
stages of growth do not bring this factor into play. Realism requires that we recognize its pervasive character, but not to the
extent of denying that a community of love and encouragement
can inhibit its expression and prepare the soil for repentance.

In short, compulsion and voluntary learning go hand in hand

[30]For example, R. S. Peters, ed., *The Concept of Education* (London: Routledge & Kegan Paul, 1967).

at all stages of education, and compulsion is most effective when the learner forgives the intrusion and volunteers to abide by it. The attitude toward education which we awaken all too rarely is that represented by the child whom Anna Hogg found alone, and crying bitterly, on a school playground during classtime. When she asked why he was crying, he replied through his tears, "'Cos I was let out early for being good."

Although we cannot avoid compulsion in some aspects of learning, it is doubtful whether we could ever lead the child toward autonomy without exercising to the fullest degree whatever free thought and action the child was capable of at each step of the educational process. Where compulsion drives people into roles such as "teacher" and "taught," voluntarism fosters personal relationships; where compulsion limits the teacher's mandate to enlightenment, voluntarism permits him to press for commitment; where compulsion prescribes a common route in the things necessary for all, voluntarism allows exploration of one's own special interests.[31]

Hence a twin study to this one would turn the coin over and see what conditions of freedom favored the voluntary element in education. I choose here to perform the harder task of exploring the conditions which make an element of compulsion necessary so that we might be realistic about our negatives before embarking on the more positive quest, and thereby be protected from the kind of utopian thinking which has appeared in a great deal of humanistic writing.

COMPULSION: WHERE AND HOW MUCH?

It is time now to put to work the general principles we have been discussing, and to consider at what points in the educating process it is appropriate to apply various forms of compulsion. It is not an all-or-nothing question.

Attendance at School. This is the obvious area to consider first. It is worth remembering that in most countries where schooling

---

[31]I have explored the differences between the ethical matrices of compulsory and voluntary learning in my book *Called to Teach* (Sydney, Australia: Angus and Robertson, 1971), pp. 26f. and pp. 74-78.

is compulsory, the legislation only dates back to the nineteenth century.[32] Admittedly, both parents and society have applied strong pressure throughout history to ensure that children acquired the knowledge and skills to prepare them for their places in society. But when such customary sanctions were given legal status, there were two ominous effects: one was a certain loss of parental freedom, and the other was the equation of "education" with "schooling."

For the first of these—the loss of parental freedom—the case is the same now as it was then. Irresponsible parents need to be constrained for the sake of their children; it is a lesser evil that they be compelled than that their perverse use of their freedom should deprive their children of educational help. There are still continuing debates about the best age for a child to begin compulsory education, and the best age for him to end it. White leans to seven as the lower limit;[33] I incline to four. Some states in the U. S. lay down eighteen as the upper limit; Bereiter suggests thirteen.[34] The right solution, I suggest, ultimately depends on developmental factors such as mental and emotional maturation, and on how much learning we believe should fall within the core of compulsory curriculum.

The second effect—equating "education" with "schooling"—is more troublesome. In the late sixties, Illich and Reimer launched a scathing attack on the school as an institution, and would have had us replace it with various voluntary educational services.[35] Edgar Friedenberg touched on the issue of children's rights, a recent concern in educational literature, when he reminded us that the child "cannot petition to withdraw if the school is inferior, does not maintain standards, or treats him brutally. . . . His position is purely that of a conscript."[36] And some years ago Paul

[32]A book which relates this phenomenon, as it occurred in Britain, to the deschooling literature is David Wardle's *The Rise of the Schooled Society* (London: Routledge & Kegan Paul, 1974).

[33]White, *Towards a Compulsory Curriculum*, pp. 71f.

[34]Bereiter, *Must We Educate?*, p. 52.

[35]Illich, *Deschooling Society*, and Everett Reimer, *School Is Dead* (New York: Penguin Books, 1971). A useful discussion of children's rights as Christianly discerned is contained in C. Glenn Cupit's "Children's Rights in the International Year of the Child," *Journal of Christian Education*, Papers 64, June 1979, pp. 25-40.

[36]Quoted in *The Experience of Schooling*, ed. Melvin L. Silberman (New York: Holt, Rinehart & Winston, 1971), p. 224.

Goodman suggested that older adolescents be given educational vouchers which might be redeemed by imaginative projects or travel schemes as well as by schooling.[37] Undoubtedly, many of the criticisms now directed at schools could be minimized if schools made a greater effort to be community-related; I also suspect that there will always be some things which are better learned through enlightened institutionalized procedures. But there is force in the argument that we have put too many of our educational eggs into this particular basket, and need now to explore other avenues of guidance as well, particularly for the adolescent. Youth services, part-time work release, independent study and travel—all of these merit investigation in relation to the recognized need for compulsory education.

Determination of Aims. Compulsion is also inevitable with respect to the aims of the educational agency, whether it be a school, a learning exchange, or an external study program. Anyone who takes it upon himself to provide some form of educational guidance for learners has to that extent dictated the way in which needs will be met. When the learners are children, much has to be determined in advance, even by the most progressive of educators. Few are content merely to be child-minders.

Hence all educational agencies sponsored by like-minded people exercise at least a benign compulsion. Decisions about the values and policies of the institution are made initially by the sponsors, and thereafter color the experiences of the learner. If it be objected that one cannot be prescriptive about values and policies in a pluralistic society, then the result is not "progressive education" but no education at all.

It is true that the larger the sponsoring community, the more difficult it is to get sufficient agreement to lift the educational agency's tone above mediocre compromise and pseudo-neutrality. This is one of the most cogent arguments for getting away from highly centralized state school systems and finding better forms of community involvement.

The "Hidden Curriculum." Whatever is done to clarify the aims and purposes of the educational agencies in a particular commu-

---

[37]Paul Goodman, *Compulsory Miseducation* (New York: Penguin Books, 1971), p. 57.

nity, the result will fall far short of what we desire unless we recognize the effect of what many are now calling the "hidden curriculum." This is the experience of institutional living itself, which for many students far outweighs the effect of the formal study program. As Silberman reminds us,

> For well over a thousand hours a year, students are urged to follow routines and procedures, to get along with each other, and to respect adult authority. Every day, student's actions are praised and criticized, their movements are directed, and their values and beliefs are shaped.[38]

Unlike some radical critics, I do not consider the institutional effect a necessarily bad thing, because I believe that some institutionalization of human associations is always inevitable and needful. But for too long we have ignored the possible educative or miseducative impact of the institutions as such, and I fear that relationships today between administrators, teachers, and students leave much to be desired.

I said earlier that there were good reasons for espousing democracy as a form of government, subject to certain reservations. This remark has to be modified for educational institutions, in which the immaturity of children militates against anything like equal representation. But participation, feedback, and cooperative effort; student representation on policy committees; the granting of genuine status to voluntary activities of the kind usually termed "extra-curricular"—these are all ways to bring the hidden curriculum to light and to make it serve true educational purposes.

There are also lessons here for those who train teachers. If we are to overcome the common insensitivity of teachers to the way children really feel—a syndrome caused, perhaps, by the strains of mass teaching, and teachers being themselves at the bottom of a professional hierarchy—then our training must include a critique of schooling and exposure to such sensitive teacher-writers as John Holt, Herbert Kohl, and Edward Blishen.[39] I cannot shake off the seriousness of Jesus' remark in Luke 17:1-2:

---

[38]Silberman, *The Experience of Schooling*, p. 1.

[39]See such books as Holt, *How Children Fail*; Herbert R. Kohl, *36 Children* (London: Victor Gollancz, 1968); and Edward Blishen, ed., *The School That I'd Like* (New York: Penguin Books, 1969).

Things that cause people to sin are bound to come, but woe to that person through whom they come. It would be better for him to be thrown into the sea with a mill-stone tied around his neck than for him to cause one of these little ones to sin.

This is the Christian valuation of a child!

The Formal Study Program. Originally, in the era of compulsory education, this was a very rudimentary grounding in the four R's—reading, "'riting," "'rithmetic," and religion. By degrees the literary-academic subjects of the grammar school filtered down into the public school, were liberalized, and now dominate public school systems. In fact, learning activities outside the literary-academic mainstream still have a hard time achieving status. More recently, Australia has swung toward the American policy of multiplying elective studies and reducing the core subjects. England is also on this road, and John White's professed reason for arguing in favor of a compulsory curriculum was his conviction that his country had gone too far.

I believe that if we recognize that freedom has a knowledge condition and a developmental condition, then we will see the need for a compulsory study program, though my caveat is that this should go hand in hand with voluntary learning activities, which would include electives.

The problem, then, is to identify the components which should be compulsory. There are a number of good recent proposals to choose from, including White's, and I have elsewhere made plain my own attitudes on this question.[40] I would, however, add one further remark. If the spiritual condition for freedom holds true, then it is imperative that the compulsory study program include studies of the human quest for meaning, for purpose and redemption, as it is illustrated in history, literature, ethics, religion, and art. In saying this, I am not necessarily committing the school to timetabling subjects by these names; better teaching strategies may be available. I am merely identifying dimensions of learning which must be incorporated in the compulsory teaching-learning activities of the school.

[40]See Hill, *Called to Teach*, Chapter 3.

The Uses of Assessment. A fifth area in which compulsion operates is that of assessment. There is no question that effective teaching depends on continuous feedback; contention arises over the way that feedback is obtained and how the information is used. Traditionally, schools have assessed students by giving them written examinations that grade them like apples; eighty percent of them have been told that they are unfit for the university. A proportion of these have been given a piece of paper saying that they have finished school. Though we may well question the compulsion exerted on the school by the requirements of universities and employers, we have yet to have twinges of conscience about the ethics of the school's passing on confidential information about students without their knowledge or consent.

If it is the business of an educational institution to foster autonomy of mind in its students, then assessment must be for the student's benefit. This does not mean that he may not be given a true picture of his level of attainment in comparison with his peers for advisory (not competitive) purposes. The fact is that we need constantly to engage in "reality testing" to see where we stand in relation to the external world. But it should be the student's prerogative to decide what is done with the information thus obtained.

The point is not that assessment should not be compulsory: if a school has a compulsory curriculum, then assessment is an integral part of its operation. Rather, the point is that assessment should be in the student's interest—and it rarely is. Critics like Holt and Glasser have identified the devastating side effects of learning dominated by fear of failure and ridicule, and we have yet to learn from them.[41]

One may still wonder why assessment should be compulsory at all. Why not let the students simply learn in their own way, and leave it at that? The answer is that assessment for purposes of diagnosis and feedback not only reinforces the learning achieved, but also exerts a discipline over the student which is characteristic of both knowledge and skill. The child who is kept at his piano practice after his initial enthusiasm has waned is learning that the rewards of satisfying performance come only to those who sub-

---

[41]Holt, *How Children Fail*; and William Glasser, *Schools Without Failure* (New York: Harper & Row, 1969).

38   mit to the discipline of the subject. Ignorance, immaturity, and perversity could deprive him of this essential lesson, were he not compelled—with compassion, one trusts—to achieve the standard required. One suspects that the dissatisfaction that many feel with the "declining standards" in schools that stress "grade-point averages" is due to amateurish assessment policies which disguise the standard required for mastery, and disregard the students' need to experience the *disciplines* of knowledge and skill. Having leaned for too long on external assessors interested only in applegrading, we as a professional body lack the skills to encourage mastery-learning.

POSTSCRIPT

There are some who would say that my defense of a certain amount of compulsion in education has simply reaffirmed the right of the ruling class to dominate society through its schools. But I would refute this charge on the grounds that I gave qualified support only to those compulsory strategies which appeared likely to further the goal of bestowing more effective freedom on the learner. I also stressed the desirability of exploring the extension of the voluntary principle in education in such ways as enriching electives, community involvement, and student participation in decision-making in the school. It should be evident that many of the compulsory strategies currently employed in schools do not have my support.

On the other hand, I have tried to show that some of the most popular apostles of freedom in education are doing children a disservice by basing their claims on naive and utopian visions of man. One cannot help agreeing with Bernard Shaw's reaction to Rousseau's claim that children are born free. This, said Shaw, was "the most flagrant lie ever told by a sane man."[42] Biblical teaching makes the contrary point that man is not only born into the ignorant and dependent state of infancy, but born into an environment spoiled by his species' inclination to choose the bondage of sin—an inclination which cannot be explained purely in terms of ignorance or class oppression.

---

[42]Quoted in Paul Nash, *Authority and Freedom in Education* (New York: John Wiley & Sons, 1966), p. 8.

The liberation of the growing child can be achieved only by an educational policy that faces up to these realities, and accepts the fact that formal education by itself can only aim for personal autonomy. But this cherished autonomy brings us to the threshold of the substantive choices which really determine whether the learner will be slave or free: hobbled by the caprice of his own warring soul, or liberated by a resolve to seek first the kingdom of God and His righteousness.

2 Students or Subjects?

"Which should I put first—
relationships or subject matter?"

FOR some reason it is easier to think in twos than in threes or fours. Perhaps this has something to do with the brain having two hemispheres, or with the binary functions of computers, or with the lack of a species between sheep and goats. Whatever the reason, we tend to polarize issues and to reduce the available options in thought to two, especially when we are dealing with the triangle of forces in teaching mentioned in the introduction. The teacher mediates the world to the learner. He has to be concerned with both his subject matter and his client, the student. Yet educational theory and practice seem to veer toward either pole in preference to establishing a justified balance.

On one side are those who place the main emphasis on *content*, urging us to impart knowledge to our students and to develop in them a capacity for cool, critical thinking. This, they say, is the best service we can provide to students. On the other side are those who emphasize *relationships*, stressing the need for the education of feeling and warmth in personal interaction, and professing to be relatively uninterested in which particular subject facilitates the process.

It may seem that I am exaggerating a difference of emphasis. I shall argue in Chapter Seven that the clash is at a more fundamental level than this, but it will be enough to show here that the situation is as I have described it, and then to argue for a Christian view which reconciles epistemology and personality,

This chapter is an expansion of an editorial on "Subjectivity and Subject-Matter in Teaching" in the Journal of Christian Education, *Papers 62, Aug. 1978, pp. 3-10.*

and thereby helps the classroom teacher to keep an appropriate
balance in her curriculum.

THE CURRICULUM DUEL

On the side of objectivity we may range an impressive amount
of work done recently by cognitive psychologists and philosophers. Much of the curriculum reform which took place after
Sputnik in 1957, including such impressive projects as "Chem
Study" and the "new mathematics," drew on the empirical work
of such people as Jean Piaget, Jerome Bruner, Nathaniel Gage,
and David Ausubel. In the philosophical sphere British philosophers in the mold of R. S. Peters and P. H. Hirst have made a
sophisticated case for establishing critical rationality as the aim of
education. Each represents an enlightened attempt to rise above
the dry intellectualism and rote learning of old-style schooling by
encouraging the skills of logical and autonomous thinking, and
a heightened awareness of the heritage of knowledge on which
our present culture is built.

Echoing this at a more popular level has been the public clamor
over allegedly declining standards in the basic skills, and pressure
to institute wide-ranging "competency" tests. The country that
led the world in breaking the grip of external examinations and
uniform compulsory syllabuses is showing many signs of revert-
ing to similar devices under different names. Teachers wishing to
stress objectives of a more affective kind are hamstrung by the
fact that the famous Bloom's Taxonomy,[1] though very serviceable in the cognitive domain, is weak and confusingly classified
in the affective domain. In particular, it appears to relegate to the
area of emotions all questions of willing, valuing, and adopting
commitments.

On the other side is a strong tide of opposition to such trends,
those who argue that students are being subordinated to social
requirements, domesticated for future industrial recruitment and
exploitation. Many advocates of "open education" call for more
informal learning styles, sensitivity training, and encounter groups.
The "free schoolers" and "deschoolers" seek to dismantle edu-

---

[1]*Taxonomy of Educational Objectives:* volume 1 on the *Cognitive Domain*, ed.
B. S. Bloom et al.; and volume 2 on the *Affective Domain*, ed. J. L. Krathwohl
et al. (New York: David McKay, 1956 and 1964 respectively).

cational authority structures and to re-define the relationship of teachers to learners. Thus Carl Rogers declares that he wants to be known not as a teacher but as a "learning facilitator."[2] His humanistic psychology—so-called because it emphasizes with Abraham Maslow the development of "human potential"—stresses the non-directive guidance of learners, encouraging them to gain self-confidence and self-identity from defining their own learning tasks and cooperating with others.

Both camps can present plausible arguments, and the Christian teacher feels alternately pulled from one side to the other. He knows that God has given us minds with which to explore a created order sustained by the far greater mind of God. He also recognizes that it is by virtue of his capacity to *know* God and to respond voluntarily to Him that the special status of the human person in the created order is distinctively affirmed. What draws the Christian teacher to the teaching of subject matter is his conviction that it speaks ultimately of God, and students deserve to hear His voice in general revelation.

But the Christian teacher is also disturbed at the ease with which cognitive theories subtly declare a preference for the brighter child, the high academic achiever. He sees assessment, which was meant to help the learner appraise his progress and diagnose his difficulties, turned against those learners whose grades put them at the lower end of the normal curve. He sees senior teachers in the high school competing for the talented and motivated seniors who are allegedly so much easier to teach. He sees rationalism elevated to messianic status, and balks at textbooks which predict inevitable social reform through the application of scientific intelligence and objectivity.

He turns, then, to those who focus on the human subject, for this also seems right on biblical grounds. We were made for community, and find fulfillment in activities which give us a sense of significance and friendships which affirm our own identity. The classroom should be a happy social setting for learning, for rewarding initiative and curiosity. In God's eyes each individual is different, each has equal worth, and so it should be in the classroom. Let the children learn, at their own rate, what they choose to learn.

[2]Carl R. Rogers, *Freedom to Learn* (New York: Charles E. Merrill, 1969), pp. 153f.

But again the Christian teacher is forced to pause. Those advocates of free schooling and open education who are in the "new humanist" camp turn out to be grounding their theories on a strong belief in the innate goodness of the liberated individual, and in his tendency to healthy adjustment. They seek to free him from all external constraints, whether those constraints be mass measurement for educational purposes or objective morality and knowledge for personal direction. They discount the solid gains of past scholarship in favor of sensitivity groups and self-exposure through personal journals. The Christian teacher sees strong-minded humanist teachers enticing students into self-seeking relativism and disloyalty to homes in which God is honored, using their personal influence to invade the privacy of the individual. Given also that the emphasis is on affective education and the nurture of attitudes and relationships, the student is even more vulnerable to manipulation than in those situations in which people are merely trying to transform his cognitive processes.

THE DUEL OF THE HUMANISMS

Seeing some truth and some distortion in each emphasis, the Christian teacher will want to find a theoretical position which holds each in balance and helps her to develop a consistent teaching style. Since good scholarship and research are the handmaids of theology, irrespective of the persons responsible for doing them, the teacher is justified in looking to the wider world of human thought and investigation for clues. But when she does, she finds that the divisions persist. On the one side is the relentless march of objectivity, bringing order into the investigations of scientific fact: in the seventeenth century launching experimental science in physics, chemistry, engineering, and astronomy; in the nineteenth, entering the biological and medical sciences; and in the twentieth, coming into human studies. In contrast to the speculations of ancient thinkers and the dogmatisms of religious writers, here, it seems, is tested knowledge, free of individual bias and subjective whim.

In the light of such evidence, the Christian teacher might be inclined to feel that her respect for subject matter has been confirmed, were it not for three things. First, the exponents of objective, scientific knowledge often have a habit of dismissing, with a sneer, the claims of religion and universal morality as prescientific superstitions. This is hardly consistent with the biblical view of knowledge, nor is it an attitude based on scientific inquiry, but rather on prior assumptions. Second, the archpriests of organized intelligence seem either hell-bent on enlarging our powers over atom and gene while treating conscience as an epiphenomenon not worthy of their attention or respect, or bemused at the unforeseen consequences of their "pure" research.

Third, the Christian may well deduce from such facts—and from the tendency in recent philosophy of science to stress the subjective and ideological elements in scientific method—that knowledge is not a neutral terrain but a theoretical construct which varies with the observer, even in such "neutral" studies as atomic physics. It is easier to see that this is so in the *human* sciences, in which entire disciplines seem dependent on the particular view of personhood preferred by their major exponents, whether it be the rational egoist of some economists, the reacting organism of behavioral psychology, the class-conditioned man of Marxist sociologists, or the gullible consumer of industrial psychology. By the time one encounters the advocacy of "relativism," used, though in different senses, in fields as various as modern physics, anthropology, ethics, and art, the stage is set for a reaction of extreme subjectivism. Objective knowledge is a myth, a deception practiced on us by various vested interests. Let us affirm the only area of knowledge in which we cannot be challenged: the inner life of the subject, me.

This, in fact, is what happened to many sensitive thinkers in the early years of this century. Old-style humanism was never so sure of its command of truth and value as when it marched into the twentieth century glorying in the progress of rationality, scientific discovery, and technological advance, and prophesying the creation of a just and rational society. Liberal Christianity followed meekly after, acclaiming the same vision and adapting the doctrine of the kingdom of God to it. The most advanced nations then proceeded to grab for power through colonization and outright war! The First World War was a terrible blow to idealistic thinking, and had a traumatic effect on many young intellectuals in Europe. Their gods had betrayed them, and human beings had been slaughtered and tortured for temporary territorial gain. Politicians had decreed it, the ecclesiastical establishment had blessed it, and the scientific establishment had supplied the weaponry for it.

One emergent kind of thought was the passionate revolt against objective knowledge which is often referred to as "existentialism." In various ways poets, philosophers, and playwrights pointed out that in developing systems of thought, theories of reality, and structures of society and industry, our masters had deprived the individual of significance. It had then been logical to treat him as gun fodder in the pursuit of some grand political objective. But the grand designs were meaningless if they robbed the individual of meaning, for society is composed of conscious beings, not cogs. The existentialists claimed that human thought had taken a wrong turn when it chose to detach knowledge from the knower, exalting the observer's stance of the objective scientists. It had overlooked the need for persons to live by meanings which mattered to them, and it had undervalued subjectivity.

United though they might have been in their protests against dehumanizing trends in the military-industrial society, existentialists were far from agreed on the antidote. Some went in a religious direction, others in an anti-religious direction. Religious existentialism focused on the inwardness of faith, and stressed experience at the expense of doctrinal belief. In an extreme form, this could lead to a "mythologization" of belief (misleadingly termed "demythologization" by Rudolph Bultmann) whereby Christians, for example, would be urged to abandon attempts to defend the historicity of the Bible and of events like Jesus' resurrection, and to grasp instead the subjective truth of the "Christ of faith" who brings new life to the trusting believer when he gives up his resistance to the ground of his being. Religion, this viewpoint claims, is a matter of subjective states sustained by archetypal symbols and objective dogmas about God and the world.[3]

Others, like Sartre and Camus, went in an anti-religious direction, viewing organized religion as just another discredited

[3]I do not want to imply by this critique that I see nothing good in existentialism from a Christian point of view. While I view it as inadequate to account for the historicity of the Christian revelation, I believe it can provide correctives to excessive rationalism in our approach to faith and doctrine, and illuminate the central importance of relationships with God, others, and ourselves. Notable contributors at this level include Kierkegaard, Buber, and Marcel.

authority system. For them, no answers to life could be found outside the consciously existing individual. Each must make his own meaning, choosing for himself what he should become. There are no absolutes—only the absolute freedom of the individual to affirm his own worth in an absurd universe.

The early atheistic existentialists were very conscious of the loneliness and homelessness of the individual, pitted, as they saw him, against an uncaring environment. Where the Christian existentialist might speak of a sense of alienation from God, the source of all being, Sartre thought the human predicament lay in the fact that, as conscious beings, we are capable of looking for meaning, but there is in fact nothing outside to correspond with this quest, unless it be other questing conscious beings. With them, we may perhaps share our sense of estrangement, of rage at meaningless suffering and calamity. Karl Jaspers saw value in "limit situations" like fear, suffering, death, and guilt insofar as they drive us to explore our hidden reserves of spirit and, it is hoped, help us find the courage to be.

It took a worldwide economic slump and another world war to alert the transatlantic "New World" to the profound questions that European existentialists were asking about the industrial great society, and perhaps the fact that no alien bombs had fallen on American soil kept the perception of the human predicament from having its full impact. Some Christian theologians, notably Reinhold Niebuhr, did get the whole message, but Niebuhr was, after all, equally indebted to the Lutheran view of man's predicament. Americans of more humanistic temper, however, chose to see hope for man in his own inner resources, and a new humanism developed, typified by the "human potential" movement. In an even more diluted form, the hedonism of the Playboy philosophy and the counsel to "do your own thing" have worked out, American-style, the implications of atheistic existentialism for daily living (and, it may be added, for some theories of classroom management).

Where, then, has our Christian teacher arrived in his quest for guidelines to help him properly assess both subjectivity and subject matter? His dilemma appears to derive not merely from disagreements between curriculum theorists and psychologists, but from a schism between world ideologies. The emphasis on rationality and science is most loudly espoused by old-style humanists, the emphasis on subjectivity and self-expression by new-style humanists. In either case, the Christian teacher sees some things to commend, and some to oppose. At the level of technique he can learn much about how to facilitate learning of both kinds, but he needs a unifying vision of man and the world which neither humanist ideology can supply. Can the biblical world view meet his need at a sufficiently specific level?

It is probable that adequate answers will be forthcoming only if we begin the inquiry further back, at the presuppositional level of epistemology, or theory of knowledge. What is the Christian theory of knowledge, and is there a place in it for personal knowledge and knowledge through personal encounter? A preliminary charting of the terrain may begin with two great biblical affirmations.

THE EXTERNAL WORLD IS GOD'S CREATION

To the Christian, the affirmation that the external world is God's creation is a familiar truism, but it provides the scholar with a presupposition of great power. The first verse in the Bible makes the point that "in the beginning God created the heavens and the earth." The creation of man in God's image comes much later in the account, at verse 27. Hence the real world is not in the mind of man; it is a prior creation which confronts that mind, which is external to it. We cannot simply change the world by changing our minds about it and about the laws which we think govern it. We are in many ways subject to it, and attain greater freedom only by understanding it and learning to achieve our ends in ways which are in harmony with it, rather than in ways which try to ignore or oppose the constraints of nature. This is as true of the psychological behavior of persons as it is of the industries which exploit natural resources. We are dealing with a natural *order*, not a pliable flux of random entities.

The scientist who humbly searches for order is bound to have more success than the one who arrogantly expects his data to fall in line with human will, whether expressed in a theoretical paradigm or an engineering project. Wonder, humility, a willingness to let oneself be tutored by the facts, and a delight in "thinking God's thoughts after him" are the appropriate motivations for the study of subject matter, and lead to a respect for *what is*, or truth, which many post-Christians are losing. They will learn the less for their rampant subjectivism. "It is the glory of God to conceal a matter; to search out a matter is the glory of kings" (Prov. 25:2), and they shall reign as kings who give God the glory.

In epistemology, this provides us with a Realist base in the philosophical sense that what we observe is not merely "all in the mind" but *out there*. There is something to be known outside ourselves. At the same time, it was *put there* by God, so our Realism is not Materialism; the material world is not all there is. Christian Realism acknowledges the origin of all things in the mind of God, and this accounts for the possibility that we, who are made in the image of God, can think thoughts which *correspond*, to a greater or lesser degree, with the reality "out there." This has sometimes been taken as justification for an Idealist's view of the world, causing us to stress that what we *know* is our own mental activity. But this does not do justice to the "otherness" of the external world, which is not God but which, like us, was made by him. "In the beginning was the Word," but "through him all things were *made*" (John 1:1, 2). In C. S. Lewis's choice phrase, the external world is, *like us*, one of God's creatures.

WE ARE MADE IN GOD'S IMAGE

What distinguishes us from the rest of the known creation is that we *know* we were made, and this introduces an element of discontinuity in the range of created things. Our bodies make us part of the natural order, but our awareness of our self as thinker, of the world as other, and of God as maker points to a nonnatural endowment which is the image of God in us (Gen. 1:26, 27). Thinking God's thoughts after him, Adam is represented as *naming* the animals (Gen. 2:19f.); this is not mere *Nominalism*, which in philosophy is the view that we attach convenient symbols to experienced events to aid discourse, even though these symbols do not necessarily correspond to the real nature of what is "out there." It is a Realist activity in the sense that the names are meant to bear information about the natures of the events.

This distinction is readily illustrated by quoting the debate in contemporary philosophy of science: on the one hand are those who say that scientific models or paradigms are handy fictions which serve the purpose of stimulating research, and on the other hand are those who say such models are approximations of true descriptions of reality which, it is hoped, are getting progressively closer to the real.[4] The second viewpoint is easier to sustain in the physical and biological sciences than in the human sciences, because in the former our power to manipulate inorganic and organic materials is increasing by leaps and bounds, whereas in the latter the complexity of the phenomena has so far prevented us from developing sufficiently comprehensive paradigms.

One of the special problems of the human sciences has been the attempt to ape the natural sciences with regard to observing events from the outside and analyzing observations by statistical processing. Such procedures are helpful, but when applied to persons they can lead to over-emphasis on determined behavior and mass phenomena. In reaction to this, there has recently been increasing interest in "ethnographic" studies, i.e., studies which rely heavily on a participant observer's study of the perceptions of individuals sharing in an event (such as a meeting or a "lesson" in a classroom). Like the older introspective psychology of Freud, such inquiries assume that how people see the world and understand their own situation is at least as important as what an external investigator of their situation might observe more objectively.

There is, however, a tendency for such studies to deny the value of objective appraisal—of the event and of their reports— as though the only reality in such situations *is* the experiences of the participants themselves, about which no general statements linking them to more pervasive theories of action can be valid or helpful. This is a reaction into subjectivism which the Christian Realist will avoid, while not underrating the importance of personal experiences and decisions. For he knows that it is also because of the *imago dei* in us that we can rise above the plane of strict causality and make choices which modify the external world.

IMPLICATIONS FOR SCHOLARSHIP

Such considerations have at least two consequences for the world of scholarship, where Christianized input is badly needed at the

[4]See, for example, Thomas S. Kuhn, *The Structure of Scientific Revolutions* (Chicago: University of Chicago Press, 1968); and R. Harré, *The Philosophies of Science: An Introductory Study* (London: Oxford University Press, 1972).

50   epistemological level. First, it is becoming clear, particularly in the social sciences, that personal beliefs inevitably influence the direction of scientific theorizing, often functioning as axioms in the system—that is, as propositions which are not questioned in the theory because the theory presupposes them. They are the framework within which theorizing and experimenting proceed. This is not something to be deplored, because it helps to give point to our inquiries as we strive to cope with the welter of phenomena. But neither is it something to be ignored in the interests of proclaiming the virtues of objective knowledge. Bias is only insidious when it is camouflaged. Christians are not alone in having distinctive and ultimately unprovable beliefs about the world; we are all believers, and scholars should be obligated to lay their ideological cards on the table when they set out to investigate phenomena.

Second, there is hope that a more satisfactory theory of knowledge will arise in scholarly circles than the mechanistic and behavioristic views which have had such a protracted reign in recent centuries. This theory will accord higher status to the processing functions of the observing mind, and to the truth claims of speculative thought as well as experimental result. It will not, however, fall into the trap of excessive subjectivity, which loses confidence in our ability to know anything for certain, because it will affirm the reality and constancy of the external world as well as the observing mind. Steps along the way to such an epistemology include Michael Polanyi's exposition of "personal knowledge," the massive analysis of "insight" by the Catholic scholar Bernard Lonergan, and the studies by the evangelical philosopher Donald MacKay of the relationship between brain and mind.[5]

It is reasonable to expect a resurgent Christian contribution in these matters, for we affirm a belief in an order of things created by God, who is in himself a community of persons who delights in communicating with the persons he has created, and calls upon them to turn from their old ways to serve the living God. Such affirmations provide an exciting presuppositional framework for

[5]See, for example, Michael Polanyi, *Personal Knowledge* (London: Routledge & Kegan Paul, 1958); Bernard Lonergan, *Insight* (London: Longmans Green & Co., 1957); and Donald MacKay, ed., *Christianity in a Mechanistic Universe* (London: InterVarsity Press, 1965).

an epistemology which does justice to the existence of persons in an ordered world. Some scholarship of this kind is emerging in Roman Catholic and Reformed circles respectively, but one could wish that these writers would contribute more often to the secular journals in which the scholarly running is currently being made.

IMPLICATIONS FOR THE CLASSROOM

On such an epistemological foundation, it will be possible to build many applications to educational theory and practice. A few possibilities can be foreshadowed even now.

First, the teacher will have a respect for *the transmission of knowledge*. It is part of our worship of God to find out more about the world he has made. In most schools, the pressure of facts to be learned and the instrumental spirit in which they are studied (e.g., to get better grades or to gain entrance to a university) kill the urge to glorify God. Alternatively, teachers may use the occasion to glorify man the discoverer, encouraging an arrogant and exploitative spirit. Christians will transmit knowledge with respect and joy, as an invitation to worship and self-discovery. The instrumental pay-offs of knowledge will not be ignored, for it is also Christian to be concerned about the relief of the human condition, but this will not obscure the intrinsic testimony of knowledge to him who is the Truth.

Second, the teacher will emphasize *the status of the knowing mind*. This will cut at least two ways. On the one hand, the teacher will show students the limitations of reason, as evidenced by the need to use simplified models of reality which inevitably take some things for granted. The study of such subjects as biology, religion, economics, and history will include critique of paradigms and discussion of presuppositions and alternative viewpoints. On the other hand, the teacher will show students the powers of thinking persons, as discoverers and theorizers, to come to terms with the external world and to expand their dominion within it. This calls for more than the nurture of patient reason and cool logic, for the creative process also involves hunches and insights, tests and checks. The teacher will also draw students' attention to the inseparability of theoretical reason and moral responsibility, for the expansion of our understanding and power invariably raises afresh the age-old questions of whether to use them for good or evil purposes.

This last point has been memorably driven home by Reinhold Niebuhr:

> Human history is indeed filled with *endless possibilities*; and the Renaissance saw this more clearly than either classicism, Catholicism or the Reformation. But it did not recognize that history is filled with endless possibilities of *good and evil*.[6]

No area of study in the curriculum outflanks the moral question, and none may be taught as though that question were irrelevant.

Third, the teacher will bring balance to the consideration of *the complementary personal dimensions of knowledge*. The knowing mind is capable of many kinds of awareness of the external world, and each adds its quantum of value to the fulfilled life. Science and technology, preoccupied with the *means* to improve our material condition, have been so glorified in the present century that they have crowded out the relevance of the *historical* perspective, the tone imparted to living by *aesthetic* experiences and productions (even in scientific investigation), the sense of *moral* responsibility, and the *religious* quest of the spirit. Most teaching concentrates on learning for recall and cognitive operations, bleaching the curriculum of multi-dimensional appreciations of the phenomena studied in each subject. The Christian teacher will bear in mind that there will be times, in any unit of work, when rational inquiry is uppermost, times when aesthetic savoring is paramount, and times when practical application is important. In this way knowledge Christianly perceived ministers to persons in their *being* as well as their *doing*.

Fourth, the teacher will develop *person-centered teaching methods*. She will, for example, respect the processing minds, different in each sudent, which address the subject matter she presents with different mental sets, different levels of competence, and different styles of thought. Some students will tend to be more analytic, others more integrative, others more practical, others more person-oriented. Not only will she try various methods to cater to each, but she will value small groups as one way in which the

[6]Reinhold Niebuhr, *The Nature and Destiny of Man*, II: *Human Destiny* (London: Nisbet & Co., 1943), p. 160.

children may share their gifts and help each other to overcome weaknesses. Many of the suggestions of those advocating open and informal schooling are valuable at this point, provided that the teacher does not confuse means with ends, and deny the importance of knowledge to the person.

Another of her goals will be to encourage personal confidence and compassion, for she will understand that children are not only minds but embodied centers-of-consciousness, with motivations which outstrip the acquisition and application of knowledge. Her methods will affirm her students as persons and strengthen the community. She will prefer self-paced learning to sheep-herding. She will aim to enable each student to experience *mastery* of one learning task before moving on to the next.

Fifth, the teacher will undertake *assessment for the student's benefit, not the machine's.* As suggested in Chapter One, there is a tendency to see students as units on a production line that need to be graded for deployment in the social system. The Christian does not deny the need for evaluation of progress, for the individual needs to see himself in relation to the external world and to adjust his expectations to the necessities it lays upon him. But the teacher must help preserve the student's sense of self-worth by helping him find a place in that world, not implying that he has no place (through prediction of unemployment) or at best a despised place (low-status employment) in the social order. For while it would be foolish for the teacher, in an excess of subjectivity, to blind the student to the necessities of survival and the realities of his own strengths and weaknesses, it would be criminal if, instead, the teacher in an excess of objectivity crowded the student out of his personal world and left him feeling stripped of significance.

WHO IS EQUAL TO SUCH A TASK?

Looking back at what I have written, I can understand that any fellow teacher reading it might well react with the words of Paul: "Who is equal to such a task?" (II Cor. 2:16). But there is no call for pessimism. I have not forgotten the pressures which confront a teacher closeted with a class of students for hours each day. Yet even now such a teacher has to develop procedures of control and instruction according to advice received from his original training institution and from colleagues. He is already making constant decisions about how to adapt his methods to make the situation more manageable.

In this chapter I have sought to revise that advice so that it has a Christian emphasis, meant to raise the *Christian* teacher's level of consciousness. It is not just a question of how many tricks of the trade one knows, but in what light one views the overall situation and the persons in it. Anyone can borrow a trick that works, but the way in which he uses it is determined by his long-term intentions.

For example, let us suppose that a mathematics colleague recommends seating students in rows, each row headed by two of the best mathematicians in the class. The idea is that students with problems will consult their row leaders, thus obtaining counsel from their peers in terms they will probably be better able to understand. If the row leaders encounter problems, they can consult the teacher who, for the rest of his time (when he is not introducing new processes to the whole class), is able to maintain comfortable supervision over the class. A teacher may adopt this suggestion for any number of reasons. He may be lazy and wish to minimize his own workload; he may be elitist in spirit, and wish to give his best attentions only to the most gifted; he may sincerely wish to help less able children by using their peers as intermediaries; he may value the interpersonal cooperation which the technique encourages. Not all these possibilities are compatible with each other, and each will impart its own slant to the actual way in which the teacher implements the scheme.

As teachers we are making such decisions about procedures all the time. Under pressure, we react to the question "How shall I do this?" with habitual responses we have developed or adopted from others. The success of this chapter is to be measured not by a sudden transformation of our classrooms, but by the degree to which it may have shaken the secular humanist frame in which our training may have been set, and produced in us a more critical consciousness regarding the values which our teaching procedures actually enshrine and reinforce. Without this, our professional behavior may be promoting a hidden curriculum of anti-personal or anti-knowledge values which would horrify us if we were aware of it.

3 Religious Studies

"Is it possible and desirable to teach religion in schools?"

OUGHT religion to be taught in schools? I revive an old question for two reasons. One is that it is not a live issue for many Christians teaching in both private and public schools, and I hope to show that it ought to be. The other is that despite the intense debate which surrounded the issue in the nineteenth century, and again within the memory of most of my readers, it cannot be considered settled while so many variant answers are given in actual practice around the world. In some countries it is compulsory in public schools to teach the faith of the majority culture, whether it be Catholic, as it is in Spain, Protestant, as it is in Norway, or Islamic, as it is in Pakistan. In other countries the teaching of religion is prohibited, whether for ideological reasons, as in communist regimes like Russia and Albania, or on purportedly ethical grounds, as in the United States. In still other countries the religious pluralism of the society is reflected either in released time for dogmatic instruction by visiting clergy, as it is in New Zealand and Australia, or in comparative studies of two or more religions, as it is in many British and some Australian school systems.[1]

Behind most of these ongoing policies (excluding those which prohibit religious instruction) lies the assumption that religion *can*

An earlier version of this chapter was published in the journal Religious Education, *75 (Nov.-Dec. 1980), 659-666.*

[1]Australia rates a double reference because some states have a dual system whereby legislation provides for *both* general religious studies within the secular curriculum and released time for "special R. I." by visiting clergy and other accredited nominees of religious groups.

be legitimately taught in the context of general education. Against this assumption must be set the arguments of those who deny such a possibility on conceptual grounds. They claim that the notions of "religious instruction" and "general education" are mutually exclusive. If such people are right, then what is going on in most countries around the world outside the communist bloc is illegitimate and anti-educational. I am prepared to concede that this may be true in a number of instances (as it very likely is in relation to many other curriculum studies, too). I will maintain, however, that it is not inevitable in the nature of the case that the teaching of religion betray the spirit of education, and I will attempt to remedy defects in much current logic in order to show how it can enhance the curriculum.

What I shall call the humanist objection may be represented in the form of an alleged dilemma. One horn of the dilemma says that if "religious education" is understood to mean teaching *about* religion, in the sense of conducting a neutral and objective examination, then we will miss its essence, which is experience from the inside of commitment to a particular religion. Such an education will not, therefore, be "religious." If, on the other hand, we mean the teaching *of* religion, in the sense of entering subjectively into the faith framework of a particular religion, then we will be effectively evangelizing or indoctrinating rather than educating. That is the other horn of the dilemma. *Ergo*, there can be no such thing as religious education.

For a genuine dilemma to exist, it must be the case that only two alternatives exist, and that each represents an unacceptable option. In this instance, I believe I can show that the argument rests on a misunderstanding of commitment and an incorrect belief that subjectivity and objectivity are pure states of mind which exclude each other. I will argue that it is in fact possible to teach about religion in a way that is consistent with modern conceptions of education.

Having shown that we *can* teach religion in schools, I will then turn to the question of whether we *ought* to do so—i.e., whether, as committed Christian teachers, we would want to see religion taught, and in what way. Earlier I noted that both Russia and the U.S. exemplify the policy of prohibiting the teaching of religion in public schools. It is odd that they should agree on this, given the different standing of religion in their respective cultures. I will argue that failure to include religion in the curriculum is a reverse kind of indoctrination, and at the very least deforms the educational experience.

There remains the question of how far the committed teacher would want to see his own religious beliefs promoted through the religious studies program of the school. Many Christian teachers feel that another dilemma is created by the tension between their professional obligation to give children a better cognitive awareness of their cultural options, and their personal incentive to win others to Christ.

Some try to make the problems go away by saying, in effect, "If I can't teach *my* faith openly, then better that we teach nothing." Hence they, too, come down on the side of the U.S. solution. Others come down on the opposite side and resolve to find ways to teach from a stance of faith, even if it means forsaking the public school to work in a private school sponsored by Christians. I will argue that neither response is an adequate expression of Christian witness in one's profession, and that there is a plausible third way to respond.

THE ANATOMY OF COMMITMENT

The first matter to be cleared up is the faulty view of commitment which underlies the humanist objection. Humanists regard commitment as something non-rational, an emotional gesture toward a God whose existence cannot be proved, which then determines the way one will see life and the world thereafter. Once one has willed the leap of faith, *then* one understands the language and beliefs of those who share the commitment. Looked at from the outside, religions enshrine speculations about the cosmos which can neither be proved nor disproved, but which meet the psychological needs of their adherents. To be on the inside, one must accept these speculations as true and live by them without allowing critical doubt to operate. One may rationally explore the implications of these beliefs, but one may not subject the beliefs themselves to rational inquiry.

Such is the account given by a number of modern philosophers.[2] Two intuitive observations challenge its plausibility. First,

[2]See, for example, those quoted in Roger Trigg, *Reason and Commitment* (Cambridge: Cambridge University Press, 1973), chaps. 2 and 3.

the denial that critical doubt can have a place in the believer's experience does not seem to square with the facts. One may concede that there are religious people who suppose that they are required to repress doubts, and who guiltily smother any questions that come to their minds about what they believe. In such a view, doubting is a mortal sin. But there is no lack of religious teaching[3] to the effect that faith, far from depending on the repression of doubt and a refusal to face up to the intellectual challenges presented by others, should be built on the recurring *conquest* of doubt through reflection that re-affirms its plausibility, and on renewed commitment to action predicated on the belief. In all the high religions, faith is represented neither as blind devotion nor lame belief, but as reasonable commitment.

Second, the converse denial that faith is operative in the humanist stance is also implausible. The objector talks as though he himself is free of commitment to unprovable beliefs because he lives by the dictates of critical reason and a willingness to doubt everything which cannot be empirically verified. One school of philosophical thought, the logical positivists of the 1920's, attempted to apply this logic with full rigor to research: they believed that only those propositions which could be tested experimentally were "meaningful." The demise of this viewpoint was brought about by several criticisms, one of which was that the verification principle *itself* could not be verified in terms of its own criteria. It was actually a value-loaded prescription of what was to count as knowledge, and a very limiting one at that. In other words, the logical positivist was committed to the prior belief that the ultimate reality is the observable, physical world. In this faith he proceeded to dismiss all talk of religion, art, morality, and politics as epi-phenomenal, that is, as not bearing on the central facts of life. It should be noted that the positivist commitment was not unintelligible to outsiders, whose criticisms eventually secured its downfall, an occurrence which suggests that they did not need to hold that commitment themselves to understand it.

Not all humanists were or are positivists, but I have taken this

[3]See, for example, citations and arguments in Os Guinness, *Doubt* (London: InterVarsity Press, 1978).

extreme example of an anti-metaphysical stance to show that the humanist could no more avoid metaphysical commitments than anyone else. All thinkers, humanists not excepted, argue from starting points in thought which involve beliefs about the cosmos, or the way things really are, that are not provable in the precise empirical sense. To this extent the humanist, too, is a man of faith.

I offered the previous two points as intuitions because they arise from informal rather than controlled observation of the way in which believers and self-professed non-believers actually operate. More compelling, perhaps, is the claim made by Roger Trigg in *Reason and Commitment* (Chapter 3) that the nature of commitment has been misrepresented by philosophers in the humanist tradition. Commitment, he maintains, is "acting in accordance with a belief." An act which was not dependent on some prior belief, however minimal, could not properly be said to demonstrate commitment, but would fall into the category of unreflective behaviors. The belief underlying the act may not be known to be true, but the actor must at least believe it to be true. It is implausible to suppose that any person would act on a belief he knew to bear no relation to fact. He must suppose that it has some purchase on reality, even if verification in the precise empirical sense is lacking because of the all-embracing nature of the belief, as in the case of a belief in the existence of a personal God.

A second point Trigg makes is that whereas commitment logically implies belief, the reverse does not follow. One may believe something intellectually without acting on it. If this were not so, it would not be possible to distinguish between the two concepts. Furthermore, it would not be possible to entertain provisionally as true claims the beliefs advanced by another person, nor to be persuaded to change one's own beliefs. Those philosophers who talk as though we develop forms of thought and systems of explanation which are incomprehensible to those who have not entered into the respective commitments from which they spring— creating, as it were, different intellectual worlds—are hard put to explain conversions by persuasion and disagreements that persist after mutual comprehension has been established. Yet such experiences are common.

The misunderstanding of commitment owes not a little to the way in which subjectivity and objectivity, as we saw in the previous chapter, are polarized in much modern writing. The first horn of the dilemma, it will be recalled, was the claim that one cannot study commitment without sharing the commitment. It is alleged that learning *about* religion through the study of its history, sociology, psychology, belief claims, and so on, lacks the flavor of personal participation in its form of life. It is worth noting in passing that the objection is not confined to the issue of religious education. This will have a familiar ring to those acquainted with the philosophy of social science, for increasing numbers of writers in that field argue that one cannot study a culture objectively but must first become a participant to really know what is going on, whereas others claim that to do so is to lose the power to report scientifically—that is, objectively—on what one discovers by this means.

Underestimated in such accounts of human awareness are the capacities of imagination and empathy, which are compounded of both objective and subjective elements. Imagination enables us to entertain worlds that are not yet, view-points that are not our own. Empathy enables us to enter into the feelings of others, to resonate with their responses to situations (without necessarily sharing or *sym*pathizing with their values).

If it were not possible for A to appreciate B's point of view, challenging though it might be to A's own point of view, how could A meaningfully represent his own view as alternative? If it were not possible for B to enter imaginatively into A's state of mind and will, how could B understand enough to trigger a change of commitment? It is true that people are sometimes converted to the view of another more by his personality and conduct than by anything he says to them about his beliefs, yet a change in commitment comes only after a change in belief, however limited in scope; and this belief in its turn is entertained as true only after being first entertained in the imagination at a stage when it is thought to be probably not true or not important.

It is sometimes said that our capacity for imaginative empathy can enable us to entertain *some* of another person's beliefs and feelings, but not his total commitment, especially when this total commitment is to a God who allegedly reciprocates with gestures of relationship such as the imparting of assurance and answers to prayer. But, given the individual's capacity to entertain in imagination some of the experiences of another, and given the individual's own similar range of experiences, there seems to be no good reason to stop short at certain kinds of commitment and to say the "willing suspension of disbelief" can go this far, and no further. If one actually considers the number of ways in which human beings seek out and enter into vicarious experiences—through conversation, literature, drama, history, and other expressive arts—it seems a universally characteristic preoccupation.

So far as the limiting case of an alleged personal relationship with God is concerned, the believer would be the first to admit that this is not experienced through face-to-face encounter of the kind familiar in human interaction, but through such mediating channels as one's feelings and rational reflection, external circumstances, the study of Scriptures believed to be authoritative, and the counsel of others. Such channels of experience are severally available to the inquirer, who may then imaginatively test the construction placed on them by the believer. I may not know X, whom Y, let us say, knows and loves deeply, but I have in my life most of the building blocks of such a relationship, which enable me to understand what such a relationship means to Y, even though I myself am not directly involved in it.

There is one situation in which this will not be so: if in fact my previous experiences in life have been so impoverished that I lack sufficient building blocks. Sensory and emotional deprivation in infancy may stunt my natural capacity to empathize with other persons. Restricted intellectual and social intercourse may leave me prey to the ignorant fear that creates barriers of prejudice between me and people who are in some way different from me. Also, it is a contemporary commonplace that we now live in a complex and pluralistic society which requires of the child a more substantial initiation into the social reality than most home environments alone can provide.

Such defects of background in children entering school are not damaging merely with respect to the teaching of religion. Every subject will suffer to a greater or lesser degree.

Such considerations become, in fact, primary reasons for that form of benevolent interventionism in the life of the child which we call the school. The school has the responsibility of teaching children *about* the culture they are entering, and doing so in such a way that they understand it imaginatively as well as intellectually. The modern concept of education is predicated on the assumption that they can reason, feel with others, and exercise imagination. The subjective-objective dichotomy is blurred by this specification, for to *know* about many things—perhaps most things—one must be able to empathize with practitioners and imagine possibilities, which requires the joint operation of our capacities for both subjective and objective awareness.

All this, be it noted, falls short of personal commitment, failing to satisfy the condition that it be a settled disposition or tendency. All that we require is the ability to "try on" a commitment as an actor might assume the role of a character in a play, or the reader of a novel become absorbed in the thoughts and following actions of the main characters. Everyone, it seems, has some measure of capacity in this direction, and most can be given help to improve it.

It is necessary, however, to ask whether children will be as competent to "put off" as to "put on" the commitments exhibited in the classroom for their inspection and understanding. The answer is partly developmental, depending on when they become capable of abstract reasoning. It is probable that children will uncritically, and often inconsistently, adopt many commitments demonstrated to them in their junior years, whether in religious studies, or literature, or any other subject. Indeed, given that there is an early need to shield developing persons from the more unsettling aspects of pluralism and to provide them with a psychological "home base," as it were, of agreed commitments, it is desirable to collaborate with some of the unverifiable beliefs embedded in their respective home allegiances, on the understanding that at a later stage in their general education these beliefs will be subject to critical reflection.

Yet there *is* a kind of experience, akin to commitment, which can be observed in a single lesson, and which *does* encourage us to believe that even learners who are quite young can distinguish between emphathizing with a commitment and actually adopting that commitment themselves. Borrowing from C. S. Lewis something he wrote specifically in his capacity as a professor of literature, I will call this "reception."

The notion is most easily illustrated with an example from the field of literature, though its implications run throughout the curriculum, even affecting the sober "mechanics" of doing arithmetic. Consider what is involved in teaching poetry. Memory brings back the teacher whose method consisted of dictating biographies of poets and instructing students to write "metaphor" next to line 15 on page 22 for use in the examination. Little better were those teachers who welcomed a new poem as a chance to "critically analyze" it in the spirit of a dog worrying a stripped bone. Lewis denies the critic the right to analyze the piece until he himself has first "received" the experience it has to offer, submitting himself to the message being mediated before reflecting on what it means and how well it is communicated.[4] Similarly, there is more to the experience of "doing" mathematics than applying rules and formulae, more to science than following the steps of the classical experiment. The feeling of being on the inside of the mode of experience is an essential moment in the process of coming to understand it. Analytic appraisal complements this feeling, just as Buber acknowledges the complementary alternation of I-Thou and I-It in building personal awareness.[5]

Thereafter, the learner is free to decide whether he will make his new knowledge the ground of a more enduring commitment to that kind of experience, extending the moment of reception into a disposition. R. S. Peters, also talking about initiation into the public forms of experience, appears to expect that to really understand will be to *care*, or to be motivated by a "rational passion" for that form.[6] At best, however, his argument might establish that a disposition had been fostered to *use* a particular form of discourse correctly when appropriate, but this would not

---

[4]C. S. Lewis, *Experiment with Criticism* (Cambridge: Cambridge University Press, 1961), pp. 18f., 88f.

[5]Martin Buber, *I and Thou*, trans. Ronald Gregor Smith, 2nd ed. (New York: Charles Scribner's Sons, 1958), *passim*.

[6]R. S. Peters, "Education as Initiation" in Peters, *Authority, Responsibility and Education*, 3rd ed. (London: George Allen & Unwin, 1973), p. 107.

64   necessarily entail a disposition to *value*, in terms of life priorities, the exercise of this mode of awareness.

In summary, I have argued that teaching about religion is possible without relapsing into indoctrination, and therefore the dilemma supposedly inherent in the notion of religious education is resolved. Between the polarities of acquiring knowledge and embracing commitments we have interposed a third pedagogic outcome, "reception," through the exercise of empathy and imagination. I have not used the word "sympathy," for this is a term cognate with commitment, whereas empathy is cognate only with understanding. The argument has therefore progressed comfortably within the boundaries of the liberal-democratic concept of education. Teaching about religion is possible: it is a strategy focusing on cognitive awareness, and even our moves to emphasize the subjective element more strongly remain within the broad program of developing awareness and understanding.

CURRICULUM PRIORITIES

This question now arises: Given that we *can* teach religion as part of the general education we offer through schooling, *ought* we to do so? The answer will depend in the first instance on whether our general theory of curriculum holds that anything at all should be regarded as compulsory for core study. While some free-school theorists would leave the choice of subject matter almost entirely up to the child, I argued in Chapter One that we may in good conscience accept the need to prescribe some of the child's early learning experiences.

Most contemporary attempts to identify the studies which should form the core of general education acknowledge the need to come to grips with the phenomenon of religion in culture and personal life. Whether they approve of it or not, even secular theorists are forced to recognize that some understanding of religion is necessary if we would hope to comprehend adequately the records of history and literature, and to grasp the motivations behind much of what happens today in the ethical, social, political, and technological spheres, as well as in art. Any genuine attempt to help students become cognitively aware of the world they have to cope with must include an encounter with the phenomenon of religion. For good or ill, it is there. Christian theorists, of course, do not doubt this, but ambiguity creeps into their stance when it is a question of recognizing the legitimacy of dealing with other religions besides Christianity in the curriculum of religious studies. (I shall return to this point later.)

Religion is a many-sided phenomenon, and it must be studied in ways which do justice to this fact. In a justly celebrated analysis, Ninian Smart has pointed out that there are at least six dimensions involved, and neglect of any one will distort the educational presentation.[7] A "social studies" approach may pick up the *social* and *ethical* dimensions of religion, but neglect the others. An approach through literature or art may detect the *mythical*[8] and *experiential* aspects that Smart lists, and perhaps the *ritual* aspect to the extent that it takes on dramatic forms, but neglect the others. All of the dimensions so far mentioned will be inadequately comprehended if due regard is not given to the *doctrinal* aspect, that is, to the belief-claims generating a characteristic and rationally worked-out view of the world. Without necessarily endorsing all the details of Smart's "phenomenological" approach to the teaching of religion, which in my view strives excessively for the appearance of value-neutrality, we can at least use his dimensions as a checklist with which to evaluate any claim of adequate representation of religion in the curriculum.

The foregoing observations may be expected to make sense to developers of curriculum for general education, whatever their personal stance. That in itself is reason enough for the Christian teacher to support the case. But he has additional reasons. First, he understands better than many of his contemporaries that man does not live by bread alone, but by convictions about the meaning and purpose of life. Deprived of either, he deteriorates. It is arguable that many people in the well-fed societies of the West have characters stunted by the seductive consumerism of an affluent and materialistic society which discourages them from asking basic questions about the point of it all. Marcuse identifies a serious ailment in such cultures when he speaks of the one-dimensional false consciousness of such people, who live for the

---

[7]Ninian Smart, *Secular Education and the Logic of Religion* (London: Faber & Faber, 1968).

[8]Whereas liberal theologians would label many biblical passages as myth, the evangelical scholar would affirm that there is little, if any, deliberately mythological material in the Scriptures. This category would better suit other religions.

present in the shallow confidence that their fragile, materialistic paradise will never break down or fail to make them happy.[9] But the root of their malady lies deeper than the capitalistic economy on which Marcuse blames it. It taps into a stratum of personal identity and sense of significance which the mass mentality does not accommodate. The Christian teacher should welcome the opportunity to help children to achieve that objectivity regarding contemporary lifestyles which religious world-views and critiques nourish.

Second, the Christian teacher must believe that any student alerted by religious studies in school to the ultimate questions of meaning, purpose, and redemption will be that much more ready to take seriously the efforts of Christians in the larger society outside the school to commend to him the logic of their stance— i.e., to evangelize—and that much better equipped to tell the phony from the well-founded. This suggests that the teaching of religion in the public school, if done as competently as the teaching of other subjects, will, from the Christian's point of view, have a *pre-evangelistic* function. There is nothing unethical about this. So long as such an outcome is seen as a welcome side-effect rather than an explicit educational objective, it stands as testimony to the objective validity of the Christian view of the world. Because it fits the facts, it calls the soul.

If, however, the curriculum offers no religious studies at all, then the effect will be to evangelize implicitly in favor of the view that religion is peripheral to the serious business of living. Far from being value-neutral, such an outcome highlights the absurdity—in a society as indebted to the Judeo-Christian tradition as the U.S.—of that society's prohibition on religious studies in the public schools. If the humanist objector espouses this policy in preference to one which admits the study of religion and includes his stance among those studied, he is unmasked as one striving to indoctrinate others with his own belief.

But, third, provided that the Christian religion is adequately represented in the religious studies curriculum, the Christian teacher should have no fear, in terms of her own belief, about the student being exposed to other belief systems as well. For if Christianity is the truth that she believes it to be, then it can only

---

[9] Herbert Marcuse, *One-Dimensional Man* (London: Abacus, 1972).

gain from comparison with its rivals and invite belief on its own merits. This, again, is an outcome desired by the teacher which cannot be one of the explicit aims of education as such, but neither is it incompatible with those aims, since the fact that the teacher hopes for such a side effect places no pressure on the pupil and no restriction on the development of a critical consciousness with respect to the phenomenon of religion.

EXTRA-CURRICULAR ACTIVITIES

If the school does its proper job of making students aware of the religious dimension in human nature and experience, particularly as it finds expression in their own immediate community, then the task of the witnessing Christian beyond the formal classroom setting will be made that much easier. And opportunities in the community at large are as numerous as they are voluntary. Some opportunities even exist on school premises, in cases in which school authorities have the wisdom to recognize the value of voluntary extra-curricular activities and societies to the education of their charges. Christian teachers are often insufficiently alert to the opportunity of being involved in voluntary Christian fellowships on school premises with their students and others whom they don't themselves teach in class. After all, the catchment of the public school is *all* young people of educable age in the adjacent community, excepting those (unfortunately, mostly Christian) who have been drawn off into private schools.

It is true that there are also important voluntary-group ministries to be performed in private schools and in church-based youth groups. But when the Christian teacher is faced with the issue of priorities in the investment of his own time and talents, he should ask himself this question: Who else has as good or better access than I do to the unchurched youth population gathered on public school premises? It may well be, as Chapter Five acknowledges, that the decisions he makes as a Christian parent, particularly with regard to where his own children go to school, may reflect a different set of priorities from the decisions he makes as a Christian teacher, but the question should be asked with full seriousness.

CONCLUSION

The above argument has proceeded along two fronts. First, the *possibility* of religious studies in public schools, consistent with the enlightened modern concept of education, has been demonstrated, countering the humanist objection that the very idea generates a logical dilemma. The key lies in understanding the role of reason in commitment, and the middle ground between objectivity and subjectivity. Second, the *desirability* of general religious studies has been affirmed, both from the point of view of general curriculum theory and the specific concerns of the Christian teacher. At the present time, when there is increasing criticism of the public school and its curriculum, it is fitting that the voices of Christian teachers be heard urging adequate treatment of the religious domain in the secular curriculum. The justifications which have been canvassed here have been educational, not sectarian. For the most part, these justifications should be acceptable to the profession and community at large as they struggle to improve the quality of public education.

4 *Christian Schools*

"Should I really be teaching in a Christian school?"

ONE of the best ways to detect how much Christians are swayed by their cultural conditioning is to discover their attitude toward Christian involvement in schooling. Consider the following propositions: a society must have universal schooling; Christians have a duty to try to maintain the monopoly of Christian values in public school policy, or, alternatively, they should send their children to schools controlled by Christians; school-teaching is properly one of the charismatic callings of the Holy Spirit. None of these propositions commands a clear mandate from Scripture, nor does church history speak with one voice. Yet various Christian groups today defend each of these propositions, and dismiss those who think differently with the unargued claim that "the Bible says so."

I do not want to imply disrespect for those who base their educational theory on what they claim the Bible says. I do think they are often unchristian toward the genuine outsider who would like to discuss their views with them but who cannot stomach such a blunt take-it-or-leave-it response. There has always been a strong tendency among some Christians, notably Catholic and Reformed, to disdain explaining themselves to the non-Christian man on the grounds that, being natural man, he cannot understand the things that are spiritual. In particular, since he does not recognize the unique authority of the Bible (supplemented, in the

An earlier version of this chapter appeared as "Is It Time We Deschooled Christianity?" in the Journal of Christian Education *Papers 63, Nov. 1978, pp. 5-21. Responses to this argument were featured in Papers 67, July 1980, and have influenced the re-draft published here.*

Catholic case, by the tradition of the church), what is the use of arguing? The whole debate starts there.

Now it happens that I agree, at least with the Reformers, that it does all start there. If I personally am more indebted to the Reformation than to any other theological tradition, it is because I believe it did recall the Christian mind to the primacy of biblical revelation. I, too, believe that it *is* necessary to re-align my thinking with what the Bible says, thereby loosening the grip that my cultural conditioning has on my mind. If I am then obliged to part company with the things that some Reformed writers are saying about Christian education, it is because I think that they are attributing to the Bible propositions that reflect the sixteenth-century social conditioning of the original Reformers.

BIBLICAL IMPERATIVES?

Universal Schooling. Consider, first, the belief in universal schooling. This is only a relatively recent phenomenon; for most of the human centuries no such thing existed. Its beginnings lie in the Reformation period, and Prussia and Scotland were its early leaders, with other Western societies following suit only 150 years ago. Why did these countries support this belief? Was it because "the Bible says" there should be universal schooling?

Their stated reasons were that the Bible declares every person to be the object of God's love, and itself reveals God's will for every person. Hence all people should be able to read the message for themselves, and that requires training in literacy and religious instruction. Scripture also enjoins us to be sober, hardworking members of society, which implies a certain level of moral and practical instruction.

So far so good. But how were these things to be done? Luther charged every municipality to set up Christian public schools. Calvin was more inclined to keep church and state separate, and committed control of the school system in Geneva to the church. Declaring that Christ had instituted four special orders—those of pastors, teachers, elders, and deacons—he assigned the responsibility of schools to the teachers. It is obvious that his grounds for this view of holy orders were biblical passages such as Ephesians 4:11, in which we are told that God "appointed some to be apostles, others to be prophets, others to be evangelists, others to be pastors and teachers." Equally obvious is that he imposed greater order on these functions than was apparent in the original documents. How essentially biblical was the social structure thus generated?

Williston Walker once aptly described Calvin's political vision as "essentially the mediaeval theory of the relations of church and state."[1] It is a vision which required that society be officially Christian; that all instruction be predicated on the assumption that one's students are Christians under nurture, thus merging the separate functions of evangelism and teaching in the agency of schooling; and that *all* teaching, whatever the content, be viewed as an extension of what the Bible refers to in many places as "teaching."

Society in biblical times followed none of these dictates. Classicist Edwin Judge[2] points out that the early Christians instructed their children in matters of faith and morals at home and in the congregation, not in schools. The more affluent Christians might let their children attend pagan schools for the purposes of cultural broadening, but apparently their fear of the counter-influences of pagan instruction was not strong enough to lead them to set up rival schools. It was only in the fourth century that the church became involved in sponsoring schools for general purposes, in response, it would seem, to a desire to protect a useful social institution from collapse at a time when the civil control of the Roman Empire was breaking down. The motivation was evidently similar to that which led Christians into areas of social welfare and medical care. That is, the initial focus was not on preservation of the Christian flock but on a Christ-like concern for social need in the community at large.

By the twelfth century, medieval Christendom was in full flower, all social institutions deriving legitimation from the view that they were in effect ministries of Christ in a society of which he was officially and ideologically Lord. Even so, schooling was not a universal phenomenon. On the whole, schools provided education for leadership, and catered to an elite. The Reformation broadened the base and prepared the way for mass education,

---

[1] Williston Walker, *A History of the Christian Church* (Edinburgh: T. & T. Clark, 1918), p. 394.

[2] E. A. Judge, "The Conflict of Educational Aims in New Testament Thought," *Journal of Christian Education*, 9 (June 1966), 32f.

though still perceiving it, from the perspective of an officially Christian society, as a divinely ordained function of the church.

Today such a perspective is no longer plausible. The development of rival belief systems, begun by the Reformers themselves when they forsook Catholicism, has progressed to the point at which society can only survive on an agreement to tolerate differences in belief while at the same time looking for opportunities to work together at a practical level to maintain dialogue, economic viability, and caring services in the community.

Does this include agreement on the desirability of universal schooling? We noted in Chapter One that there are some who contest the point, but I argued there that society has developed to the stage at which it cannot do without some such provision. Nevertheless, writers like Illich have been justified in drawing our attention to the way in which we have been culturally conditioned to think everything depends on the school. Since the introduction of compulsory schooling in the early stages of the Industrial Revolution—a revolution which is still going on and is causing great changes in lifestyle and social organization—the role of the school has steadily expanded.

At first the common school was given the task of imparting basic literacy and reinforcing social controls through moral and religious instruction. Then it began to provide secondary education and widened academic and vocational options. Next it began offering vocational guidance, health care services, and psychological counseling. Today it is being asked to provide courses in human relations and pastoral care, and it is also being blamed for juvenile delinquency, long hair, and bad spelling.

Why do we insist on thinking that all worthy social goals and, at a higher remove, the objectives of Christian nurture, may be appropriately laid on the school? It was not so in biblical times, and the mounting evidence of research is that in fact schools cannot, by their very nature as institutions of compulsory mass education, whether under state or church auspices, do all that is asked of them in areas of moral, social, and religious commitment. They have a humbler, though essential, role to perform: helping children—*all* children, for I take a biblical view of human worth—to cope with their technological, pluralistic environment. I support universal schooling, but not as the universal panacea.

Christian Monopoly. The second proposition was that Christians have a duty to try to maintain the monopoly of Christian values in public school policy. The key word in this proposition is "monopoly." Here again, biblical sanction is lacking. Certainly the Old Testament presents us with the picture of Israel as a theocracy controlled by its spiritual leaders, but the Bible as a whole teaches us three things about this experiment in theocracy: first, that it did not work because the present world order is not ready for it, and the medieval period teaches the same lesson; second, that the *new* Israel is a dispersed fraternity acting like sprinkled salt to savor the whole community; and third, that the truly Christian members of society, as against those whose allegiance to the church is nominal, are *always* a minority whose testimony is most compelling when it cannot compel but only influence.

Christian Garrison. But this is a hard saying, especially when one is thinking of one's own children. And it seems even harder to Christians who look nostalgically to past eras of Catholic or Protestant Christendom rather than to biblical times and the social conditions under which the faith first flowered.

Even if public schools were well run and ethically managed, it would still be a hard saying, for one knows that the seesaw of fashion in scholarly theories and the voice of the natural man in literature and the arts often run directly counter to the things Christians hold most dear. But it becomes an even harder saying when one discovers how many public schools are in fact places of moral anarchy and biased teaching, when one sees community values squeezed out by bigness and bad management, when individuality is sacrificed to the Molech of comparative measurement. Hence some Christians are embracing as biblical the alternative proposition that parents should send their children to schools controlled by Christians.

As a parent, I can sympathize deeply with those who draw back from the secularized systems and industrially minded teachers of the public sector, and desire something better for their children. It is very biblical to be concerned for the welfare of one's own children.[3] One can understand, too, the urge to with-

---

[3]Some of the classic passages are Deuteronomy 6:1-9; Proverbs 4:1-9 and 19:18; Matthew 18:1-6; Ephesians 6:1-4; Titus 1:6.

draw from the larger community and to set up a Christian school. It may even be the right reaction in certain cultural settings. All I am saying *here* is that there is no direct biblical injunction to do so, and the justifications must be more indirect, weighing the salt principle against the principle of parental responsibility (if indeed they are at odds) and investigating whether in fact public schools damage religious commitment more than what I am here calling Christian garrison schools.

The Biblical Concept of Teaching. The last proposition advanced by some as biblical is that school-teaching is properly one of the charismatic callings of the Holy Spirit. How does the Bible use the word "teach" in its cognates?

In the Old Testament, the word "teach" occurs constantly in association with such other words as "instruct," "tell," "direct," "lead," "show," and "command." Classic examples are Psalm 119 and Job 1–4. The very word *tôrâ*, or "law," comes from a parent verb meaning "to teach" or "to direct." If one checks the usage of such words with a concordance, he is struck by the consistency with which the *content* of such teaching turns out to be moral and spiritual revelation. It is an activity which occurs within a community of commitment—between the believer and his Lord, or between father and son, or between the prophet and the people of God. In typical Hebrew fashion it engages both mind and will. The test of whether the commandments have been well taught is whether I live by them. The teacher is appropriately someone of the same faith who mediates the truths of God to me, not in school but in the family settings of home and church.

In the New Testament, these perspectives on teaching continue to apply. There is added, however, a dimension of special grace, or *charis*, which is needed to give life to the transmission of revealed knowledge. A kind of professional teacher, the religious scribe or "teacher of the law" did emerge in the closing centuries of the Old Testament, but he was seen as having sacrificed the spirit of the *tôrâ* to the letter, and the image of the teacher of the faith needed to be restored to its properly spiritual status. Those who aspired to teach had to be reminded that they were stewards of a gospel, requiring God's help at every point to convey it correctly and in a manner which would modify the learner's conduct. Hence it was to be seen as a grace-gift, or *charisma*, to be exercised in the setting of a body of believers; a special calling for some, but also a general ministry of all, edifying and instructing each other.[4]

The same notion—of a special calling for some, but also a general ministry of all believers—applies to the teaching associated with "teaching all nations" in the Great Commission of Matthew 28:19. This is teaching with the hope of making Christians of one's hearers, "baptizing them" into the faith.

Some of the characteristics, then, of the biblical sense of teaching are these:

1. Its context is nurture within the community of faith or direct evangelism beyond it.
2. Its content is the moral and spiritual revelation of God.
3. Its manner is both instruction and admonition, challenging as well as informing the learner's manner of life.

In short, the Bible sets forth a very special sense of "teaching," more restricted than the range of meanings familiar to us in ordinary language. Such a definition hardly seems appropriate when one talks of teaching Jimmy to swim, or Joan to ride a bike, or Jack to do carpentry, or Jenny to understand quarks and quasars. It is true that the Christian teacher inevitably finds that these more ordinary teaching roles are for him modified by his view of his pupils' status before God as persons of worth, and his interpretation of knowledge in biblical perspective, but this hardly requires that every ordinary teacher display the special *charisma* of one called by God to teach the Christian faith. That is as unwarranted a claim as saying that only those with the *charisma* of prophecy should work in the secular field of predicting economic trends.

Why does the Bible not supply us with injunctions and examples related to these other kinds of teaching? I believe the answer is that they are culturally conditioned, and concerned with matters not central to the relationship of persons with God and each other. The children of affluent people went to school in Jesus' day; the sons and daughters of ordinary people learned their

[4]This is seen in such biblical references to "teaching" as Romans 12:3-8; I Corinthians 12:29; and Ephesians 4:11.

76   work skills from their parents "on the job." Neither activity at-
tracts biblical comment.[5]

In short, the Bible is concerned with a specifically priestly and
pastoral sense of teaching,[6] whereas common usage and recent
social developments provide us with a number of other meanings,
and in particular with one secular meaning which has acquired
very precise definition as a result of the rise of compulsory schooling—that is, the sense in which we speak of "professional
teachers."[7]

In summary, then, there is no clear biblical mandate for the
establishment of Christian schools. Some important general principles affect the issue, such as the worth of each individual, the
obligations of parents, the duty to be "salt" in the community,
and—one not yet mentioned—the unity of creation as the work
of God. But starting from these baselines, evangelical Christians
may and do go both ways on the question of whether such schools
are desirable. To determine, if we can, who is more correct, we
must look beyond Scriptural evidence to the cultural conditions
which have prompted Christians to take the route described as
the Christian garrison approach. And we must not overlook any
available empirical evidence about the effects of different types of
schooling.

[5]It might at least be thought that the "schoolmaster" gains recognition in
the metaphor used by Paul in Galatians 3:24, which speaks of the law as a
schoolmaster to bring us to Christ, especially since the Greek word used gives
us the word "pedagogue" *(paidagogos)*. But the Authorized Version is misleading
at this point. Later translations more correctly depict this person as a child-
minder or guardian, not a teacher and not in a school. A benign policeman
might be a closer analogy!

[6]It is priestly in that it involves the authoritative mediation of revealed truth
to another; pastoral in that it seeks to shepherd the other in living out his faith-
commitment.

[7]I take it that it is teaching in this last sense that Illich is objecting to when
he urges us to "deschool" society. Perhaps there are things that the church, too,
can learn from Illich's prophetic diatribe against schooling. For have we not
eagerly aped the secular world in creating our age-segregated "Sunday schools"
with their standarized teaching materials, and a voluntary staff relieving parents
of their proper role in the spiritual nurture of their children? It is no accident
that many church leaders, in the early years of the Sunday school movement,
protested that such provisions were an invasion of the parental domain and
would encourage fathers and mothers to neglect their Scriptural obligations of
nurture. Should we perhaps be thinking of deschooling Christianity, or at least
of reducing our intellectual attachment to "school-based teaching" as the bearer
of the churches' hopes for the young?

What conditions are currently operative in our culture? It is easy to see that Christianity no longer provides the ideological canopy under which society operates. Our era is post-Christian. But it is less easy to see whether any other ideology has replaced it. The rise of science and technology has turned us into a means-oriented society in which the justification of any social or political policy is that it works, i.e., that it contributes to the maintenance of civil order and personal liberty. The view that Christianity has been replaced by any one kind of systematically thought-out humanism is implausible. But we may agree that our culture is vulnerable, because at its core is a value-vacuum, a lack of any agreed sense of purpose. The "free" world is also fragmented.

But what alternative is preferable? The unfree world lies at the mercy of either total control in the name of the masses, which is Communism, or total control in the name of the few, as in Fascism. Christians must surely overcome their nostalgia for the earlier benevolent totalitarianism of "Christendom" and welcome the freedom of the secular state, however fragile. These freedoms owe much to the long-standing Christian respect for individual conscience. They also pave the way for genuinely committed Christians to commend their faith persuasively in community forums where, unable to coerce, they are therefore better able to convince.

As always, Christians are at risk whichever way they turn. To speak only of education, if they obtain sufficient political influence to coerce the public schools into promoting exclusively Christian values, they sell their gospel short. For this same gospel invites every person to make his or her own response after fully counting the cost, and that includes the cost of forsaking other cultural options. Coercive Christians also invite a coercive backlash from those whose freedoms they have curtailed; when *they* get into power, they may well try to outlaw the Christians' cherished values and substitute their own. If, instead, all Christians retire into private schools to promote exclusively Christian values, then they too may be selling the gospel short, as well as encouraging the larger community to turn a blind eye to the option their protected testimony represents. If, finally, Christians stay *in* the community and stand by the common school, working for fair representation in the formation of its policies, then their testimony is that much freer of unbiblically authoritarian overtones— but majority vote may lead to policies they abhor. Whichever way Christians turn, compromise is inevitable. There is no single right answer for Christians in a pluralistic and relatively free society; each of us, *in our particular situation*, needs to weigh the possibilities for good *and* evil in whatever choice we make. Having made our choice, we will then need to work constantly to minimize the bad possibilities inherent in that choice. Those who choose the Christian school must struggle to avoid indoctrination and cultural isolation. Those who elect to support the public school must grapple with the possibility of injustice to minorities, including their own. Each of us must also live in the tension between keeping ourselves "unspotted from the world" (Matt. 5:13) and being "salt for all mankind" (James 1:27, in AV translation).

Schooling and Nurture. Three culture-related factors are also relevant to this issue. The first is the changing relationship between schooling and nurture. We may represent this as falling into three eras. In the first, there was *nurture without schooling* (I define "nurture" as the attempt to guide a person's initial development toward adulthood, according to the ideals of those who love him for his own sake.) In the first era, most children were nurtured in extended families, held together by the close-knit and uncritically accepted values and practices of the village community, and trained for work by apprenticeships on the job.

The second era was one of *nurture through schooling*. To the extent that elitist church schools date from the time of cathedral schools of the medieval era, it overlaps the first era. But it was after the Industrial Revolution that universal schooling became common. Looking for a model of what the common school should do, the legislation had available the Reformation styles of Scotland and Prussia. In them the objectives of general education and Christian nurture were amalgamated. But the acrimonious protagonists of the nineteenth century could not entertain such a close alliance with Christianity, though they did see a need to invest the school with responsibilities of nurture, being aware of the erosion of home and community life by the factory system.

So they looked to non-denominational religious instruction to help them develop moral and social values in children.

But the experiment broke down. How can a teacher of twenty-five to thirty children be in a primary loving relationship with each child for all of his formative years? What right has the state to prescribe the ideal of personhood toward which such nurture shall be directed? A pluralism of such ideals was already present in the nineteenth century, even among Christians. True, the school *has* proved to be effective in teaching facts and in creating an awareness that our neighbors can be different without necessarily being bad or inferior. But it has not proved able to significantly change personal values and commitments.

Consequently, there has been a trend in educational theorizing to see schools as being primarily responsible for enlightenment rather than commitment, and to look to other and more voluntary agencies to complete the tasks of nurture. That is, we are entering an era of *nurture plus schooling*, in which the main responsibility for nurture is returned to primary groups such as the family and friendship circles, though it is recognized that along with this goes a need for initiation into the complexities of modern society and technology which it is beyond the capacity of primary groups to provide. This development has led to the evolution of a concept of education as complementary to nurture, but not synonymous with it. Schools cannot, of course, entirely escape the obligations of nurture, for they place students in close social groups in the course of fulfilling their educational purposes. But to the extent that they, too, nurture, it is toward a general ideal of a person who is socially productive and acceptable, not toward some particular ideal of a religiously committed person.

Education and Indoctrination. The new concept of education requires us to take the view that persons are capable not only of feeling but of thinking and choosing for themselves. They need not be puppets totally controlled by their environment. But they *are* so controlled if they are not helped to understand the forces acting on them. The aim of education is therefore to help individuals to develop their capacities of knowing and feeling to the point of which they will be able to understand their world, survive in it, and be aware of the scope it provides for personal choice. This aim emerges from a variety of ideological standpoints, ranging from classical humanist to Christian. We should not be deterred by the fact that the natural man often proposes it, unless we are unwilling to grant him any part at all in the image of God. Nor should we be surprised that it is an aim on which Western humanist and Christian can agree, for it is a product of a culture heavily indebted to the Christian tradition.

What *is* surprising is that some *Christians* want to oppose it. They want to press on into determining the student's choices for him, at least in moral and religious matters, and to shield him from encountering plausible options alternative to Christianity until he is too fixed in his ways to take them seriously. They want to see him "saved" at all costs, even if the decision has not been truly his own, and even if he is thereafter unable to communicate effectively with those of other mind with whom he should be sharing his testimony.

Christians should know better, though the Inquisition and evangelism-by-formula prove that many do not. The classic encounters of Jesus with individual inquirers show that he challenged them to understand clearly what they were doing, and to assess it in the light of the society in which they lived.[8] The concept of education I am discussing focuses on the good of the individual, not merely on social conformity. It helps him to resist cultural conditioning by becoming an informed, thinking person. It encourages him to base his choices on the best evidence available.

Christians *can* work, with good conscience, alongside non-Christians who accept this more limited goal for schooling. They can also resist, on these grounds, curriculum trends to import objectives of nurture into the classroom, attempts made either by Christians fighting a rearguard action or by humanist psychologists pressing in the vanguard. Attempts to fulfill all the tasks of nurture in the context of compulsory education, whether in public or private school, debase teaching to the level of indoctrination and conditioning, and defame the biblical view of persons.

Teaching and Evangelism. Our concept of education also brings with it an implied view of a professional teacher. It is a view of someone trying not merely to instruct or impart facts and rules,

---

[8]See, for example, Matthew 8:18-22 and 15:21-28; Mark 7:14-23 and 10:17-31; Luke 7:36-50 and 14:25-33; and John 4:1-28 and 14:21-30.

or to recruit submissive followers, but to encourage rational autonomy and humane sensitivity. To do this, the teacher herself must have professional autonomy in choosing how she teaches, and a major part in saying what she teaches. Interference in a teacher's performance of her duties can be justified only on the grounds of unprofessional conduct toward students, not on the grounds that certain methods must be used or that preferences must be shown toward certain partisan points of view.

All this implies that formal education, which is needed to help all children come to terms with contemporary social realities, must be complemented by nurturing groups like homes, clubs, and church fellowships. Similarly, the professional teacher must be complemented by adult models associating with the learner in voluntary contexts. There is a toughness in the human spirit which reacts negatively to strategies of compulsion. Testing and grading in the classroom, for example, however well sugar-coated, challenge the learner's self-concept and right to privacy, and he develops mechanisms to defend his autonomy. If he senses disapproval or consistently gets low grades, then he will look elsewhere for self-affirmation. Pressed for commitment, he will dissemble to avoid incurring the teacher's wrath.

The whole picture changes when certain values for living are commended by committed persons in voluntary encounters. With the courtesy appropriate to dealings with other people, the evangelist and spiritual teacher commend their own beliefs to the other, inviting him to respond freely and without threat or bribe. Similarly, wise parents, as their children develop into separate selves, will lovingly urge but not compel, trusting in the combination of truth and love to persuade the youth. In providing the truth needed for intelligent choice, the parents will provide both for enlightenment through education in the general sense, and for teaching within the voluntary faith community.

EMPIRICAL INDICATIVES

So far I have argued that there is no clear biblical mandate for the establishment of Christian schools, but several broad principles to be weighed against each other in one's own particular cultural situation. I have also noted the current trend toward complementarity in educational thinking; schools are held responsible for initiating children into the general culture and developing in them a higher level of awareness of intellectual and moral issues, while other social agencies more appropriate to the child's personal nurture in faith and love regain their lost status in our theorizing. Such principles concern the *theory* of education. There may, however, be brute facts in the present situation which oblige us *as parents* to take short-term measures at variance with our best visions as Christians and teachers at large. Judging by the recent surge in the formation of Christian schools, many people think there are.

One writer has claimed that the movement to found Christian schools has burgeoned to such a point that it is "the fastest growing school movement in America."[9] When one remembers that population growth has slowed down markedly in recent years, this can only mean that there has been a massive desertion of the common school by the Christian sub-population. When we seek reasons for this phenomenon, three stand out.

The first is that, particularly in the southern states of the U.S., this trend has been a measure of the refusal of Christians to comply with the desegregation policies of the federal government. No doubt the federal measures were hamfisted examples of social engineering likely to bring in their wake as many problems as they solved, but one cannot escape the conclusion that for many Christians the prime motivation has been a racist abhorrence of their black—or in some cases white—neighbors which the Gospel vigorously condemns.

Second, there has been growing disaffection with the achievement levels in public schools, particularly those in urban areas. Evidence seems to be accumulating that competency levels in the basic skills and in general knowledge are falling off, though it is worth investigating other cultural factors as well—such as the influence of mind-stunting television programs, the delinquency of non-Christian parents, and the effect of soft-option electives on the will to learn—to see to what extent they affect the issue. It is also true that the more multi-cultural the composition of a school, the harder it is to program a sufficient variety in levels of instruction to give each child the continuous experience of mas-

[9]Paul A. Kienel, *America Needs Bible-Centered Families and Schools* (La Habra, Calif.: P. K. Books, 1976), p. 9.

tery and to challenge the most advanced children (who, for cultural reasons, are mostly Anglo-Saxon). But the spiritual legatees of Pentecost should not turn their back on this challenge.

Third, it is frequently alleged that a dominant ideology of secular humanism has taken over the public schools. It must be conceded that the feeble influence of Christians as salt in the world left the way clear for secular progressive theories to play a big part in the launching of universal public education in America, and confusion in the Christian mind made it possible to banish any teaching about religion from the public sector. Such failures have led to the development of a value-vacuum in public schools. It is also true that many strongly humanist curriculum kits marketed for use in schools have been welcomed by teachers because of their good technical quality. But humanism is not a seamless garment, and there are fierce disagreements in the marketplace between alternative humanist options. The proper Christian response is not to bemoan humanist initiatives but to out-play them and to do better in the area of curriculum development. Similarly, parent-teacher associations have sometimes appeared to be dominated by highly vocal humanists, but national statistics would suggest that there would be good support for strong Christian input if it was couched in terms of the general good and not only in the distinctives of Christian morality and belief.

This is cold comfort for the beleaguered Christian parent in a hostile P.T.A. environment, or with children in a school close to social disorder. I will return to this plight in the last section. The general point I wish to make here, however, is that Christians—Catholic and Protestant alike—have historically been too ready to leave the general community to work out their own salvation in education.

Some Christian parents have grouped together to establish alternative schools without a clear idea of what they wish to put in the place of the common school ethos, for merely to say that one is forming a "Christian" school leaves many necessary details unsaid, and there is no *one* Christian way to handling general education. Some people have told me that their chief concern is to reinstate religious instruction (by which they sometimes mean Christian indoctrination). Others want teachers who are more caring or who can help timid children. Still others want to keep their children out of the drug culture and believe that this is the only effective way to do so.

In contrast are those theories of education which spell out in thoughtful detail how the process is to be thoroughly Christianized, statements which give direction to many Christian schools. Of particular appeal to many evangelical Christians are the arguments developed by writers in the Reformed tradition, as mentioned at the beginning of the chapter. The sad thing is that many of these authors write mainly for the edification of Christians and, at that, Christians of the same persuasion, rather than inviting non-Christians and brethren who think differently to engage in dialogue with them. The simple rule of making fewer assertions and offering more reasonable arguments would greatly widen the appeal of such studies. At their best, they concur with the best secular theories at the point of wanting to help children to grow in understanding and sensitivity, and to acquire and accept good reasons for their faith.

Much less laudable are those Christian theories which spring from a desire to override the individual's rational caution and propel him into obedient allegiance to Christ. A prime example of this is a program called Accelerated Christian Education (A.C.E.), which is based on the use of "programmed learning," whereby the student responds promptly to short "packages" of information. If he answers correctly, he receives reinforcement; if he answers incorrectly, he is guided to sub-programs for remedial instruction.

The psychological foundation for such methods is the "operant conditioning" theory of B. F. Skinner. Skinner has no respect for the supposed faculties of critical reasoning; he assumes that the human organism is totally determined by his environment, and susceptible to behavioral conditioning.[10] A.C.E. stands in direct line of succession to those who have sought, by emotional manipulation, to obtain decisions for Christ which by-pass the individual's rational independence, but it also cashes in on the improved manipulative techniques discovered by modern behavioral psychology.

The theological underpinnings of this kind of teaching are even

[10]See my analysis of Skinner's ideology in Brian V. Hill, "Behavior, Learning and Control: Some Philosophical Difficulties in the Writings of B. F. Skinner," *Educational Theory*, 22 (Spring 1972), 230-241.

more suspect. The A.C.E. student lives in a universe of authorities and right answers. The available ideological options are boiled
down to two: "One is the Christian way of life as laid down in
God's Word and the other is the secular way of life which promotes humanistic ideas."[11] This is true in one sense, but untrue
given that many questions about the application of biblical truth
are not black and white, and untrue in the sense that calling an
educational policy "Christian" does not necessarily mean that it
is right in all respects.

It takes time for the long-term effects of a particular approach
to schooling to become apparent. Research on private community
schools in general is meager, but one fact emerging from the
American scene is that these schools tend to come and go fairly
rapidly. The individualism which brought them into being tends
to carry over: dissenting parents break away and teachers defect.
By contrast, one would expect that the homogeneity of faith in
a Christian school would foster its continuance for longer periods.
This appears to be the case. Nevertheless, I have talked to many
teachers in parent-controlled Christian schools who testify to de-
meaning master-servant relationships forced upon them by dic-
tatorial school boards, and the frequent overriding of their
professional judgment. Break-away groups are also not unheard
of, all professing to be soundly biblical in their defection.

In the long run, institutionalism takes its toll, as the older wave
of church schools testifies. The school that heavily indoctrinates
its students either loses customers or produces many rebels bitter
with the way they were pressured to conform to religious requirements. The more seasoned school draws back to a more
general definition of educational purpose such as the one supplied
earlier. At worst, it preserves its impetus by appealing to social
elitism. Certain research evidence suggests that the church school
may inoculate many students against truly personal faith by
wrongly equating it with conformity to the rules of a Christian
school. On the other hand, most readers know of individual students who have been greatly helped by Christian schools. The
note I am sounding is one of caution, not condemnation.

[11]Editorial in SPEF *Outreach* (official publication of the South Pacific Evangelical Fellowship), July-August 1978, publicizing a school run by the mission
which uses A.C.E. materials.

PERSONAL APOLOGIA

I sounded the note of caution to counterbalance the euphoria of some who advocate Christian schools. It does not mean that I am an enthusiastic defender of government schools. I have, in fact, written frequently about their shortcomings, and have urged reform. But I have done so from the inside, that is, as a Christian who has elected to witness in the public arena on behalf of fairer representation for the Christian perspective.

I am quite prepared to concede that in a cultural setting different from that of Australia, England, and the U.S.A.—the three countries in which I have had my children in school—I might feel I had to argue for separate Christian schools, or at least send my own children to them for specific domestic reasons. Such, I think, might be the case if I found myself in a country in which other religions were propagated by law in the public schools. But my present perception of these three cultures does not suggest that such defensive action is required, or that it is demanded by the integrity of scholarship. I deny that a *unified* ideology of humanism is sweeping before it both the school curriculum and the cultural climate, though I acknowledge the existence of several radical minorities opposed to Christianity who would like to do so. It is hardly the reaction of a positively witnessing Christian to vacate the arena at this point.

In one respect particularly, Christian school theory often embodies a logic alien to Scripture. It accords validity to the activity of the Christian teacher only within the context of teaching in a Christian school, the premise being that only there can a curriculum built on Christian presuppositions be sustained. Logically, then, Christian teachers who remain in the public sector are compromising their calling. But if all withdraw, where, then, is the savoring salt? And in all charity, one must also ask whether some who have withdrawn from the public school have been animated solely by this logic, or have not also wanted to retreat from the firing line of witness in the world.

My challenge to my fellow Christian teachers is to spearhead reform in the public school sector. In saying this, I admit that I am acting on the belief that I can maintain my other obligations, as a parent to my children, by the kind of home I provide and the interactions they can have in the body of believers with whom we worship, thereby offsetting the foreseeable bad influence they may encounter in their public schools. That is, I think that I can reconcile the responsibilities of being salt in the public sector of education with my responsibility to "train up a child in the way he should go" (Prov. 22:6). But more than this, I believe that my children can benefit from the resources of public education, and that their encounters with children who are different from them and with teaching that is sometimes hostile to Christianity can better prepare them for the world—if they are given adequate home and church back-up—than my attempts to shield them from such contacts. I cannot say with certainty that I would be able to maintain this stand were my children required by rigid zoning laws to attend a public school which had reached a state of lawlessness threatening personal safety. Such things are not unheard of.

But even then an option remains, one that lies between supporting a school in the public sector and sponsoring a distinctively Christian school: it is the option of leading local community action in forming a community school which, although not exclusively Christian, is outside the governmental structure. Few troubled Christian parents and teachers, it appears, have seen the possible advantage of such a strategy, maintaining as it does the Christian's salty association with his neighbors while safeguarding the institution of school policies that are fair to the positions of all the school's patrons. Let each be persuaded in his own mind (Rom. 14:5). For this is an area, Christian reader, in which biblical revelation gives us discretion rather than direction.

5 *Community Involvement*

"Should I promote community involvement in my school?"

EDUCATIONAL theory is particularly vulnerable to the influence of fads and slogans. While the fad is "in," some word with highly favorable connotations, such as "progressive" or "open," inhibits rational appraisal by foreclosing on the possibility that the position it hallows may have some faults. The word "community" has been much used in educational discussion, with much dependence on the emotional freight it carries to forestall criticism of the actual policies being implemented under this label.

There is every reason for Christians to want to rescue this word from the fate of most slogans. If it can be clearly defined, and related in an operational way to the concept of "school," then it will yield a considerably more person-centered approach to education. This chapter attempts to relate the two concepts in a way that will provide grounds for discriminating between schools that are genuinely community-related and those which, having a form of community-relatedness, actually deny the power thereof.

A second kind of harvest, I hope, will be a view of possible relationships between schools and their communities which is serviceable both to Christians teaching in Christian schools and to Christians teaching in public schools. The mere fact of having set up a Christian school does not guarantee that it will be a community school in an effective sense of the term. Conversely, the teacher in the public school may find that some of the trends he deplores may be arrested by renewing the ties between school

---

An earlier version of this chapter appeared as "Schooling for Community" in the Journal of Christian Education, *Papers 57, Dec. 1976, pp. 24-36.*

and community, and working among Christians *in* that community to enlarge their effective voice in the operation of that school. Neither ministry will be effective if the teacher does not have a clear and Christian view of the issues involved and the values at stake.

TOWARD A WORKING DEFINITION

Is it possible to obtain a reasonably neutral definition of the word "community"? No, it is not, except in a trivial sense. Whereas useful stipulations of the term "society" appear in the literature of the social sciences, making it possible for thinkers of conflicting persuasions to discuss the pros and cons of the phenomena identified by this term, the word "community" is inescapably value-loaded. The Christian will load it favorably because of convictions about the way people were meant to enrich each other, and she will also view it as a task rather than a fact, i.e., as something which rarely just happens, but must be worked for.

The root meaning of the term picks out a group of persons who have something in common. It is not enough for them to *be* together or to live in the same locality. They must be *tied* together by some shared interest or common bond of organization which has some endurance over time.

But this still does not provide a definition sharp enough for our purposes. What has been said so far applies equally well to communities *geographically* defined and to communities *functionally* defined. For example, a suburban area is a community because its houses are all tethered to the same network of electric light poles, water mains, and, if one is lucky, sewers. We all complain to the same authorities about the roads and paths that join and divide us, and we jostle against neighbors in the nearest supermarket. This is "community" geographically defined; it is an impoverished notion, a casualty of technological development. Suburban streets tend to be rows of little castles with raised drawbridges which we let down only when we venture forth in our chariots and travel *elsewhere* to our places of work, worship, and play.

Here, of course, is a clue to the second meaning of community, the functional one, which emphasizes the sharing of enduring common interests and the nurture of lasting personal relationships. In a past age the two kinds of community were, for the mass of people, largely overlapping. Now it is common for an individual to be simultaneously a member of several communities, and to operate at several different levels of personal commitment within them. A man alienated from his work may be very tenuously committed to the community of persons at his place of employment, but deeply committed to the local branch activities of his trade union; a young person may express abundant creativity in a hobby club, yet be branded dull and inattentive in the classroom.

From these examples we learn that while human persons naturally gravitate toward community, it is possible that they may become merely lost and alienated in collectivity. Sheer numbers do not create community in the richer sense to which the Christian is committed; indeed, they may overwhelm the individual and cause his retreat into a cave of despairing loneliness. One notices how this can happen in big churches in which mass devotions and liturgical forms disguise the lack of mutual identity and caring between the members—an effect far removed from the organic "body life" that the Scriptures enjoin us to lead.[1]

In mass society, many people carry their caves with them, much as snails travel with their shells, ready to withdraw behind a tough exterior whenever danger threatens. Such people are as easily discoverable in suburban villas as in high-rise apartments; the large factory breeds them, and so does many a conventional school. Martin Buber pinpoints the threat to community in our kind of society when he says:

> In the monstrous confusion of modern life, only thinly disguised by the reliable functioning of the economic and State apparatus, the individual clings desperately to collectivity. The little society in which he was embedded cannot help him; only the great collectivities, so he thinks, can do that, and he is all too willing to let himself be deprived of personal responsibility; he only wants to obey. And the most valuable of all goods—the life between man and man—gets lost in the process; the autonomous relationships become mean-

[1]See, for example, I Corinthians 12 and 14, Ephesians 4, building on such words of Jesus as those in John 15. A well-known popular exposition of the notion is Ray C. Stedman, *Body Life*, 2nd ed. (Glendale, Calif.: Regal Publications, 1977).

ingless, personal relationships wither; and the very spirit of man hires itself out as a functionary.[2]

In defining "community," therefore, I choose to emphasize the sharing of common interests. The word "sharing" does not merely imply having in common a bondage to purposes imposed from outside (I have in mind the pupil under compulsory education). It suggests that these purposes have emerged from communion between the members of the group, who legitimate what external constraints they feel they must, but who also generate such common interests and interpersonal activities as they wish.

The implied *value* in this definition is the value of "communing," one with the other. If the question is raised as to whether an individual may not be capable of functioning effectively without exposing himself to enduring personal relationships, we are bound to say, yes, that appears to be possible. Some people do manage to "keep to themselves"; they develop private hobbies, live within neat brick fences and have few, if any, close friends. It may be claimed, however, that they are only able to do so because other people embrace the duties of citizenship and preserve the individual liberty that allows them to live in this way. One may go further, given the Judeo-Christian view of personhood, and claim that such isolated individuals, however self-sufficient, are not the people they could be, were they to cherish the mutual goods of healthy community life. Of course, one does not have to be a committed Christian to take this point of view. It is part of the argument for Christians getting involved in the community that values like this are not the exclusive property of Christians, but can be their meeting ground with people of good will from many backgrounds.

Behind the Christian's commitment to this value, however, stands the belief that God himself is a personal being, in himself a community of three persons, who delights in enlarging that community by drawing to himself adopted sons and daughters. They also learn to endow each other with good gifts, expressed in earthly communities that the Scriptures describe as instantiations of the Body of Christ.

[2]Martin Buber, *Paths in Utopia*, trans. R. F. C. Hull (London: Routledge & Kegan Paul, 1949), p. 132.

A definition may get us talking about the same thing, but it cannot of itself generate a whole social theory. We need some view of the place of community within society in general if our recommendations are to bite on the social realities of today's world. It is this need which many exponents of alternative lifestyles and "free schools" ignore, propounding solutions which can only be workable for small groups who elect to drop out of the larger society while continuing to reap at least some of the benefits of technological civilization.

It may help to compile a simplistic and to some extent futuristic history of the community idea. It is a history in three eras, with the third barely begun. The first is the era of tribal communities, which reached its limit in the organization of city-states. Tribal communities combined both geographical and functional meanings of community in an all-embracing pattern of life determined by tradition and slow to change. Such communities were also hierarchical in the sense that the power to determine the community's purposes rested with a ruling group, defined by elders and complex kinship systems. On both, the city-state superimposed a *ruling class*, and required that both plebeian and patrician conform to the respective lifestyles expected of them. In short, tribal communities were localized, hierarchical, and stable.

The second era may be called the era of national collectivities. It began with the rise of nation-states and continues into our own day with the emergence of super-nations and multi-national corporations. The era is divided into two periods, separated by the first industrial revolution. In the first period, though local community life persisted strongly in many places because most industry was based in the home, national bureaucracies and the culture of cities encroached steadily and remorselessly.

In the second period, global communications and the factory system have largely completed the rout of the village lifestyle. The pattern of national collectivity is centralized, still hierarchical, and unstable. It is centralized because mass production and distribution require it, and the mass media speak for it. It is hierarchical, more so in some countries than in others, because the god of technology is a machine, and cogs in machines don't have debates with the operator about their functions. And it is unstable because the power brokers are sometimes politicians, sometimes merchant princes, and sometimes resentful masses led by aspiring power-brokers. In our form of technological society, alienation is as common among the rulers as among the ruled. Each was made for community, but collectivity has discounted persons and personal values.

The third era is more of a dream than a reality, though here and there one may observe signs of its coming. It is the era of communities-within-collectivities. Contrary to the sentiments of those who attempt to drop out of the collectivity altogether, our hopes probably depend on accepting the gains of adapted high technology without submitting to the dictation of the consumer mentality. It is not economical use of human talent, for example, to return to subsistence farming from dawn till dark in order to register one's protest against mechanistic materialism. Automation holds out the promise of freeing people to work *at* living instead of merely working *for* a living. Advanced communications networks may release us from the tyranny of uniform entertainment by the media, while increasing our access to both community-based and collective decision-making. Some people see potential gains of this sort in community-based closed-circuit television, home computers, citizen-band radio, and so on, which together may serve to revitalize community involvement.

Another portent is the growing tendency of groups to rise up spontaneously in educated societies to promote certain specific local reforms such as pollution control, urban renewal, alternative technology, lifeline services, liberation of minorities, and the formation of "community schools." The critics of the universal education movement overlook the degree to which compulsory schooling, with all its admitted faults, has multiplied the available talents of ordinary citizens. If it has reaped the whirlwind of liberation movements, that is only further proof of its capacity to raise the general level of consciousness![3]

The pattern of the third era, then, may well be federalized, pluralized, and dynamic. It will be federalized if central governments, while overseeing problems of political security and economic production, will give up their paternalistic attempts to

[3]See, on this point, David Wardle, *The Rise of the Schooled Society: The History of Formal Schooling in England* (London: Routledge & Kegan Paul, 1974), especially Chapter 6.

monitor all phases of life, and will actively and financially encourage local community involvement of various kinds. One may
hope that Alfred North Whitehead was being prophetic when,
in the fifties, he said,

> Inside the state men pursue numerous corporate enterprises
> which . . . express other aspects of their natures: educa-
> tional, charitable, creative, artistic, social. . . . Perhaps the
> function of the state thus far is to provide conditions of
> sufficient tranquility within which those more varied forms
> of activity can proceed.[4]

The pattern will be pluralized because it will be up to local communities to determine their own form of life, subject only to the
constraints of collective security and economic viability. In many
respects, the American dream has depicted this state of affairs, in
contrast to more centralized societies such as that of the West,
France, and Australia. At the same time, however, America's lead
in technological revolution has undermined the popular ideology,
and there are signs that a grass-roots reaction is building against
state and federal bureaucratization. This is clearly a dialectic in
which Christians can play a part.

The pattern of the third era will also be dynamic, because not
all communities will proceed at the same rate or do the same
things. Some may even regress from the level of enlightenment
they previously attained, and reject some of the intellectual and
practical gains they achieved. This risk is unavoidable if we cherish community for its own sake, and not merely as a contributor
to national goals. The gains will outweigh temporary losses.

This historical digression has, of course, been a slanted one,
an effort to justify in broad social terms an attempt to put the
enrichment of community at the heart of the schooling process.
Before leaving it, however I think it is interesting to note what
has happened to that important sub-community—the school—
through the three eras described.

In the tribal situation, formal schooling was limited to the
period of intensive preparation for initiation. This period mir-
rored exactly the attributes of the larger community in that it,

---

[4]As reported in *Dialogues of Alfred North Whitehead*, ed. Lucien Price (New
York: Mentor Books, 1956), p. 97.

too, was localized, traditional, and hierarchical. As time went on, formal schooling became a more lengthy business, though the benefits were usually confined to the privileged classes. When the collective era flowered, so did schools for the newer *elites*. One should note, however, that the notion of *universal* schooling pre-dated the industrial revolution, springing directly from Christian roots in Lutheran Prussia and Presbyterian Scotland, but not gaining acceptance on a larger scale until after the industrial revolution.

Today the school has assumed a dominating role in national development and social control. And, as the deschoolers remind us, our schools are generally faithful reflections of the bureaucratic, consumer-oriented, collectivist society in which we live, whether we are east or west of the Iron Curtain.

School organization also suffers from a formidable cultural lag, the most convincing evidence of which is the traditional commitment to hierarchical authorities. Given the wide range of interested parties and the professional level of training not only of teachers but of many parents, the narrow base of many school boards and other policy structures is alarming. In my experience, the extreme was probably the small Christian school system with five schools, controlled by a three-man board of lay persons answerable legally to no one but themselves. In the large secondary schools of many public school systems, individuals are lost in the climate of collectivity, and problems of social control and cohesiveness multiply.

The third era is perhaps foreshadowed by *some* of the schools which adopt the label of "community schools." Not every school which does so is actually schooling *for* community; this, according to the view I will advance in a moment, is a necessary feature of the full notion, and one which may still be absent even when there are other features present such as parental involvement and informal class arrangements. Another necessary characteristic is that the school sees itself as answerable not to the collectivity and to such bureaucracies as it creates, but to the community which directly sponsors it and uses it. That is, such a school *also* reflects the larger social pattern characteristic of the third era, and is federalized, pluralized, and dynamic. We shall put flesh on these bones later.

Given the concept of community presented earlier—namely, a group of persons drawn together by shared purposes and an interest in fulfilling them together—what are some of the middle principles needed to facilitate its functioning?

First, a minimum requirement is *social order*. A group in which everyone literally "did his own thing"—even if he avoided causing any harm to his neighbor—would not be a community, and, as we suggested in Chapter Two, would almost certainly fall below economic subsistence level in a short time. The Christian view of persons also recognizes that there is an element in human nature which lays upon government the specific task of restraining lawlessness and the drift to social chaos. In order to survive, we *must* be committed in at least a minimal sense to the maintenance of social order, be it in the family, the school, or the collectivity. But the ground rules for the maintenance of this social order may vary from the imposition of rules by an external authority to the negotiation of agreements by those inside the particular group.

Thus my second requirement is that the methods of achieving social order be such that they enhance community rather than collectivity. That is, *social order must be the servant of community purposes, not a substitute for them*. When a community grows so big or so depersonalized that administration becomes a self-sustaining operation, then the most cherished goal, and the object of any rules formulated, is efficient conformity to the steady-state. This squelches initiative, relief of oppression, and spontaneity. The number of persons in a community must therefore be small enough to permit each a meaningful sense of participation in the process of defining the goals and rules of the community. What this size should be remains an open question empirically; it is probable, however, that without meaningful sub-communities built into them, schools with more than a thousand pupils have passed the point of no return.

A second implication of this principle is that the rules and procedures developed within a community should be scrutinized constantly to ensure that they are not working against the purposes of the whole. Communities as well as schools can have "hidden curricula"—ways of doing things which are efficient but out of harmony with the aims of association—which nullify their good intentions. Think of the accumulating paperwork which organization tends to create, in preference to face-to-face nego-tiation. Think of the formalities that teachers often insist pupils observe as signs, allegedly, of respect. Think of the pyramidic model of decision-making still common in schools and busi-nesses, with edicts being passed down through a long chain of command to the worker at the bottom. There are interesting seminal thoughts in this comment by organizational theorist War-ren Bennis:

> The social structure of organizations of the future will have some unique characteristics. The key word will be "tem-porary"; there will be adaptive, rapidly changing temporary systems. . . . The groups will be arranged on an organic rather than mechnaical model; they will evolve in response to a problem rather than to programmed role expectations. The "executive" thus becomes a co-ordinator or "linking-pin" between various task forces.[5]

A third condition necessary for community to function well is *the maximization of individual freedom, consistent with the require-ments of social order.* An administrator may well find this condition inconvenient and even threatening, especially if he has a low opinion of human nature. But community can only flourish where a high opinion of human nature is assumed, one which sees per-sonal fulfillment and interpersonal relationships as intrinsic goods, and which acts on the *prima facie* assumption that, in Whitehead's words, human beings are "liable to rationality."[6] (Note that our first principle has already taken into account that human beings are also liable to perversity.)

We all know very well, of course, that people can be frustrat-ingly irrational and stubborn, and that the committees required for participant planning can be tedious and tendentious. But those who cherish community must take the gamble, accept the frus-

[5]Quoted in Lloyd K. Bishop, *Individualizing Educational Systems* (New York: Harper & Row, 1971), p. 251.
[6]A. N. Whitehead, *Process and Reality: An Essay in Cosmology* (Cambridge: Cambridge University Press, 1929), p. 109.

trations, and work for voluntary, rational inputs. Advanced Western societies should perhaps be thanking God that their present
level of affluence enables them to absorb the inefficiencies; many
other countries have yet to establish the minimum levels of social
order and economic viability which are required, and must for
the present be more managerial in their methods. Instead of being
thankful, however, we are more likely to curse those whose individual initiative—sometimes brilliant, sometimes foolish—up-
sets the smooth running of our machine. We have forgotten that
the machine is *for* persons.

The fourth condition is the *maximization of individual equality*.
I do not say the *recognition* of individual equality, because all persons are not equal in their capacities and contributions. Elitist
social theories recognize this and are quite content that it should
be so. On the other hand, many egalitarian social theories ignore
it and either develop simplistic "rational man" models or make
mindless demands for "equal representation" of everyone on all
committees. A Christian presupposition again comes to our aid:
this time the belief that all persons, though born with different
gifts and potentials, are of infinite value before God. But how,
then, are we to steer a course between unbridled elitism and unbridled egalitarianism?

The answer lies in recognizing that a community is intrinsically
educative. It is not just at school that this is so. A true community
of like-minded friends is committed to providing opportunities
for its members to grow more equal, to prove themselves capable
of bearing more responsibility. At all levels it is inviting people
to reach a little higher, to share a little more fully in the determination of policies and procedures, to bear a little more responsibility for the welfare of others in the group.

The maximization of equality also implies a fairer redistribu-
tion of resources, which social theories usually discuss under the
heading of "social justice." Egalitarians demand the equalization
of resources, ignoring the inevitability, in a dynamic social process, of inequalities re-emerging. The answer must be a dynamic
one, involving, if one has a Christian care for persons, a constant
effort to raise the weak and share the loaves. As John Rawls has
pointed out:

The natural distribution is neither just nor unjust. . . . These are simply natural facts. What is just or unjust is the way that institutions deal with these facts.[7]

He goes on to say that in his concept of justice, "men agree to share one another's fate." That remark needs a religious commitment to give it purchase, for rationality alone will not. It is also the keystone of our concept of community.

The maximization of equality is not just a principle of fairness or distributive justice; like the third condition, it, too, is intrinsically educative. There are none so unequal and unfree as those who perceive neither their chains nor the options they are potentially capable of exercising in a civilized community.

Liberal humanists are often uneasy about the paternalistic overtones of social welfare and formal education, and we do well to have qualms about what happens to these activities when they are administered by collectivities. The problem, however, is not identified by using the word "paternalistic." Indeed, although this word has recently been used as a term of abuse, it literally denotes the responsible concern of a father. This is precisely what collectivities cannot exhibit, because administrators are too remote from the individual person.

Certain social critics are currently writing nonsense about the need to dismantle the guidance services of a civilized community, including its schools, in the name of a philosophy of freedom. In Chapter One I said something to refute this trend. We may add, adapting the comment of a Canadian writer, that it is "a paltry freedom which merely removes restraints, or even provides opportunities without providing the [bases] of knowledge and [power] which [enable] discriminating choice among possibilities."[8]

Thus both the freedom principle and the equality principle, when applied to the concept of community, require that community leaders intervene in the lives of its younger and weaker members. So long as such intervention can be shown to widen

[7]John Rawls, *A Theory of Justice* (Cambridge, Mass.: Harvard University Press, 1971), p. 102.
[8]Ralph M. Miller, "Responsibility for Freedom," *The Journal of Educational Thought*, 7 (Dec. 1973), 147.

their areas of freedom and increase their life opportunities, it is justified in the name of community.

SCHOOL AND COMMUNITY

It is now time to see how the view of community we have been developing can be put to work in a theory of schooling. The easy answer is that we are to advocate the "community school." Immediately, however, ambiguities of usage crowd in. A recent survey of relevant literature by one of my post-graduate students revealed a bewildering variety of applications. A diagram may help to classify them and to point the way to an organizing principle by which they may be made to hang together (see diagram below).

The innermost circle represents *the school itself as a community*. It is easy to overlook the fact that the school itself is already a community, composed of teachers, students, and support staff, who live together for at least five hours a day during the week. This community is in operation even before we begin to think of the larger community living around the school. The larger community needs to be tactful about its involvement in the school so that it does not invade the school's inner cohesion. Taken too far, of course, this cohesion is harmful: some schools, including some of the newer private schools, become so tightly knit that they foster in their students a kind of contempt for the larger society. It is also possible for a school which encourages individualized learning in a cooperative atmosphere still to be educating its pupils to adopt the competitive, consumerist values of the collectivity. Both of these possible outcomes fall far short of our ideal.

We therefore enlarge the circle to take in the adjacent wider community, insofar as it chooses to become involved in the school. Now we have *the community in the school*. This level of involvement may take several forms. First, people may come into the school chiefly to *use its resources*. This may not affect the school in its internal operation at all, except when premises are left untidy after public use! Second, people may come in to use its resources in a specifically educational way, as *students* during normal class hours. Third, the community may enter the school by proxy through helping to provide it with *material resources*. This is a

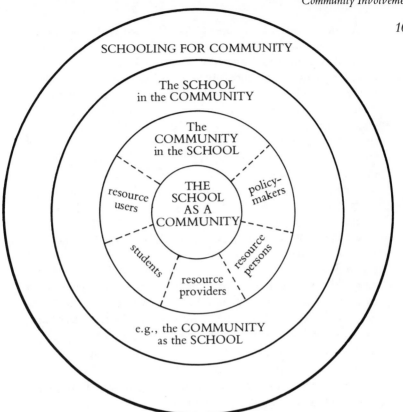

SCHOOLING FOR COMMUNITY

The SCHOOL
in the COMMUNITY

The
COMMUNITY
in the SCHOOL

THE
SCHOOL
AS A
COMMUNITY

resource
users

policy-
makers

students

resource
persons

resource
providers

e.g., the COMMUNITY
as the SCHOOL

INTERRELATIONS OF SCHOOL AND COMMUNITY

useful but low-grade involvement which often characterizes parent associations. Fourth, members of the wider community may come into the school to function as *resource persons*, working under the direction of staff in a variety of ways. This is the level at which genuine involvement begins to take shape.

The fifth and most responsible level of involvement is in *policy making*, the level at which parents and interested citizens actually participate in making decisions which will affect the day-to-day life of the school. Especially appropriate are task forces to enrich the educational purposes of the school, people who work alongside administrators, teachers, and senior students to clarify the ethos of the school and to keep it under constant review.

At this level there are three risks. The first is that lay people will unwittingly abuse the professional expertise and security of the staff unless they are guided in their input by clear agreements on their terms of reference. Another risk is that the participants will not be able to reach a consensus because of the diversity of their values and lifestyles. This is leading some Christians to despair of the public schools in some places, and to retreat, often prematurely, to schools of their own conviction. A third risk is that the consensus reached may reinforce the dehumanizing values of collectivity or a particular elitist social class. The answer to the last two hazards is for Christians to work hard at promoting a more generous vision of community along the lines spelled out earlier, and to marshal majority opinion for their views.

It is apparent that merely getting the community into the school will not automatically lead to good educational outcomes. So we try another variation on the theme, which is *the school in the community*. This is the situation in which the teachers and their students venture beyond school boundaries to explore the facilities and functions of the larger community. Taken to the limit, such a notion can overcome the concept of the school as a particular building, with the whole community becoming the school. This has happened in some "schools without walls" experiments, in which students meet in small groups in homes, local shops and businesses, and community facilities.

Such ideas have great potential, for too often we segregate students in rather sterile and artificial environments called classrooms and discourage any adults except professional teachers from entering the formal learning situation. Yet it is possible that we may be using the community merely as a "teaching aid" without effectively promoting a sense of belonging and a commitment to its maintenance and improvement. Students who sally forth to pester the public for project samples and interview data may not be developing any sympathy for the people they plague.

We therefore come to the widest circle of understanding. The concept which can pull all these possibilities together and integrate the educative activity is *schooling for community*, or, more fully, schooling for communities-within-the-collectivity. This goal would see the school as a community helping children to become part of the larger community at the request of that larger group.

School and community are then tied up in each other's futures, and the previous fragments of involvement come together.

Thus the school as a community in itself is able to focus its activities on interpersonal values and the common good, in preference to the rather self-centered emphases on competitive achievement and consumerism. Members of the community enter into the school not as outsiders but as helpers and supporters. The school goes out into the community to give genuine support to its profession that it is educating for life in the community. In short, the boundaries of the two spheres are continually blurred in the interest of strengthening ties.

KEEPING THINGS IN BALANCE

It has been suggested that a robust Christian view of persons generates a magnanimous ideal of community—an ideal, moreover, which it should not be hard to commend to a wide variety of persons who need not necessarily be Christian. The opportunity to provide leadership in the open community also broadens Christians' contact with those to whom they are called to minister and testify. The danger of introducing curricula which flout generally held values of decency and truth is reduced by a more effective community presence in school planning, and Christian lay people have the opportunity to reinforce the efforts of those on the teaching staff who are Christians. If the school and the community negotiate the disciplinary sanctions and controls which will be acceptable to all concerned *and backed up by them*, that will help reduce the sense of helplessness that both teachers and parents experience when they see some of the more exploitative elements in the wider community—including drug pushers—seeking access to school children.

What I am suggesting is that there are both idealistic and realistic grounds for promoting the notion of schooling for community. The same blend of idealism and realism is called for in designing the forms of lay-professional interaction, since it is easy for parents, given their partiality toward their own children, to become "pushy," and it is equally easy for teachers to react with defensive superiority. All forms of involvement should be clearly conceptualized, their terms of reference spelled out (including the

104   range of powers granted), and the agreement of all the interested parties obtained.

These precautions apply particularly to such delicate areas as the hiring and firing of teachers, the supervision of their professional duties, and grading procedures. There are still cases where school boards have denied professional teachers access by representative membership because they were employees to whom boards only spoke through superintendents, but this is sub-Christian in spirit. The important principle is not to follow some mechanical rule of including all parties in every committee, but to identify the directly interested parties and give them membership in proportion to their weighted relevance to the objectives of that committee.

6 The Teacher's Faith

"Dare I let my students know where I stand personally?"

FROM time to time there are attempts within the teaching profession to formulate professional codes of ethics. In general they tend to relapse into either sentimental truisms or industrial bargaining points. The Christian valuation of persons is such that the believing teacher probably has less need of this than the teacher who does not believe. Christians tend to have a genuine concern for the welfare of their students, and to be loyal to the rules laid down by school authorities regarding what is to be taught in class and how the teacher should act. Non-Christian teachers are not always so scrupulous.

In one respect, however, the Christian teacher is likely to experience more uncertainty and qualms of conscience than her non-Christian counterparts. At issue is the question of how legitimate it is to express one's own faith in the classroom and to influence pupils toward it. Non-Christian teachers without strong religious convictions won't be troubled by the problem; they'll just go on teaching subject matter as required. Non-Christian teachers with strong convictions may well share the Christian's ethical reservations about proselytizing, but there is increasing evidence that teachers with the radical views of some small minority groups think that the public schools are fair game for them, regardless of the wishes of the parents of the children they seek to influence.

The Christian teacher believes firmly in a gospel which offers

The basic argument of this chapter first appeared in Religious Education, 76 *(May-June 1981), 322-336. It is reproduced here, in an adapted form, by permission.*

salvation through Christ which he yearns to have others discover, yet he feels restrained, and rightly so, by ethical considerations of respect for the integrity of the students compelled to remain in his classroom, the wishes of their parents, and the policies of the school. Nevertheless, he retains the right, both as a citizen and as a professional person, to work for revision of the policies if he believes they fall short of what they should be. The problem is that, all too often, the Christian teacher is not at all sure what his own stance on this issue should be.

The focus in this chapter, then, is on one aspect of professional ethics—namely, how to respond to the question of how far the classroom teacher can go in revealing his own religious convictions to his students, and in seeking to influence their beliefs. The arena in view is the classroom of the public school, but the teacher in a Christian school is not absolved from thinking through the same issues. Two factors which make it just as relevant for him to consider the issues are these: (a) the existence in modern society of a plurality of belief and practice, which an adequate education (whatever the type of school) must help children come to grips with; and (b) an emergent literature on the rights of children in the context of compulsory education.[1]

I will first draw on things I have written elsewhere to illustrate three of the most commonly advocated models of teaching. These will be related to recent discussions in the general philosophy of education dealing with the question of "indoctrination" and the modern conception of "education." I will then examine in turn four possible stances which the teacher could adopt in the classroom to display her own faith, and argue for one of them as being the most desirable on *both* Christian and educational grounds.

MODELS OF TEACHING

An extraordinary amount of research evidence is available on the characteristics of teachers and the effects of various teaching methods. But the disagreements on what constitutes *good* teaching are profound. Empirical findings are there, but not an agreed view of what their sum should be. The traditional teacher, mechani-

---

[1]See, for example, J. I. Kleinig, "Mill, Children, and Rights," *Educational Philosophy and Theory*, 8, 1-16, and his bibliography; also C. Glenn Cupit, "Children's Rights in the International Year of the Child," *Journal of Christian Education*, Papers 64, June 1979.

cally pounding in facts and figures by mass production methods, is universally condemned, but recommendations on what should be the case tend to group into what I have elsewhere called the POSITIVIST, RATIONALIST, and PERSONALIST models. I shall continue to refer to these in upper case in order to make it clear that I am using the words in special senses.

The POSITIVIST model depicts the classroom as a set of variables needing to be adjusted in such a way that one variable in particular, learner behavior, can be modified in the direction that the teacher desires. Typically, research based on this model tends to itemize various teacher "acts" and learner responses which may then be correlated by using such instruments as control and experimental groups, test and attitude scales, and various kinds of statistical measurement. All behavior is regarded as being open to modification, be it mental or physical. With this model, it is pointless to talk about the *ethics* of the teacher revealing her personal beliefs; the real point at issue is whether by so doing she will *in fact* promote the objectives previously decided on. The Christian can obtain many insights from this approach to teaching, but must be uneasy that teaching is so "scientized" that ethics appears to be irrelevant to method.

The RATIONALIST model, while conceding that the scientific investigation of teaching has some value, stresses the development of rationality and self-determination in the learner. Whereas lower-order kinds of teaching such as conditioning may be needed in the learner's earlier years, the goal is to bring him into the years of formal operational thought, during which he may become capable of initiating as well as reacting to learning tasks. The key to distinctively human learning is said to be autonomous rationality, a critical awareness of one's world and the viewpoints of others. With this model it is by no means pointless to talk about the ethics of the teacher's revealing her personal beliefs, but the main point at issue is again empirical: whether by doing so the teacher will help or hinder the student's development toward rational autonomy. The biggest contrast between this model and the previous one is that the RATIONALIST approach presupposes the potential freedom of the rational person, whereas the POSITIVIST model presupposes scientific determinism. This should incline the Christian toward the former, all other things being equal.

108   The PERSONALIST model applauds the RATIONALIST investment in human freedom, but rejects the primary emphasis on critical rationality as tending to an over-investment in academic curriculum, to the neglect of other distinctively human powers such as creativity, dialogue, and commitment. It is not without interest in this connection that R. S. Peters, for example, favors that philosophical tradition which hesitates to apply the concept of "person" to the very young or the severely mentally handicapped.[2] Strongly rationalistic, his counterbalancing remarks on "personal relationships" are thin gruel to PERSONALISTS. The model also resists the atomistic approach of the POSITIVIST model, because it stresses the wholeness of the teaching encounter, the overall impact of interpersonal interaction over against reduction of the life of feeling to a sterile calculus of "affective outcomes." With this model, talk about the ethics of the teacher disclosing her personal stance is beside the point, because in fact he cannot do otherwise, even if he tries not to say anything about it. By a thousand personal cues the message gets through. The ethical point really at issue is whether one's respect and concern for the pupil's self-development outweighs the temptation to either build up one's own ego at the expense of the learner's or proselytize for one's own view of the world.

Of the three, the PERSONALIST model stands out most clearly as the one that emphasizes the need for a professional ethic, but it also runs the greatest risk of substituting emotional slogans for clear guidelines. Non-Christian PERSONALISTS especially are very likely to make ardent pronouncements about the liberty and creativity of the child without clearly defining the teacher's role, responsibilities, and limits. The risks become more evident when we relate the three models to the debate about the concept of indoctrination.

INDOCTRINATION

The word "indoctrination" came to imply strong disapproval during the period when public systems of education were moving out of the orbit of religious authorities. It was a period of ugly

---

[2]R. S. Peters, *Ethics and Education* (London: George Allen & Unwin, 1966), pp. 111-112.

argument, and the charge of indoctrination was laid constantly
at the door of church schools—particularly Catholic schools—
which were being contrasted with public schools and their pur-
ported neutrality. Today the popular myth is that Communists
also indoctrinate, whereas public schools in the Western world
continue to educate for autonomy without blinders. Critics of the
"hidden curriculum" and educational sociologists have done much
to debunk this idealistic picture. Another way to understand more
clearly what we are actually doing in schools is to study the
concept of indoctrination itself, relating it to the concept of education, with which it is apparently at odds.

Since both words, "indoctrination" and "education," appear
to have a similar linguistic form and to generate pairs of terms
like "indoctrinate" and "educate" and "indoctrinator" and "educator," it appears that they both identify processes of teaching.
Is it simply a case of the pot calling the kettle black, with the
Progressivists of the twenties saying to the church school authorities, "You indoctrinate, but we educate?" No; there is something more to it than this.

Kleinig argues that the distinctive thing about a process of
indoctrination is that it produces a person whose vision is restricted by mental blinders. As a result of teaching he holds beliefs, attitudes, values, etc., which he can no longer subject to full
rational assessment.[3] This state of affairs may have various causes.
Perhaps his teachers intended to envelop him in the cocoon of a
particular belief system by withholding information about the
alternative opinions seriously entertained by other responsible
people; perhaps they taught in a way which undervalued rational
inquiry, and led to authoritarian rote learning; perhaps they didn't
realize that they, too, were indoctrinated (perhaps indoctrinated
with the belief that capitalism was God's way of doing business),
and so in teaching the child they reproduced their own indoctrinated condition. The vital thing for Kleinig is that the result is
a stunted person, one who lacks independence and control over
his life to the extent that some of his beliefs are not really *his*, but
are implants diminishing his responsibility for his own life choices.

This account is more plausible than those which have at-

[3]J. I. Kleinig, "Educating and Indoctrinating" in *Concepts of Education*, ed.
J. V. D'Cruz and P. J. Sheehan (Melbourne, Australia: Dove Publications, 1976),
pp. 23-31.

110   tempted to locate the essential characteristic of indoctrination in particular teaching *methods*, or special areas of teaching *content*, or the suspect *intentions* of the teacher toward his students. However, though not conceptually central to indoctrination, all three factors may be causally responsible to varying degrees for inducing an indoctrinated state of mind. It is useful to ask how these factors figure into each of our three teaching models.

The POSITIVIST model seems particularly vulnerable to the charge of tending to produce an indoctrinated individual. As for method, it gives the teacher authority to prescribe what shall be learned, and then to so program the sequence of instruction that the learner will exhibit the desired terminal outcomes precisely and in minimum time. Some of the procedures will, indeed, better merit the description "conditioning," to the extent that they bypass entirely the consenting mind. It may be objected that the teacher using this model may nominate "critical thinking" itself as one of his objectives, in which case the model will escape from the net of indoctrination. Yet it is hard to see such an open-ended objective being achieved by procedures which presuppose predictable outcomes, precise teacher direction, and "objective" assessment schedules.

Yet it would be totally wrong to dismiss the model on these grounds. So resolute a RATIONALIST as John Wilson has conceded that it may be necessary at times, particularly in the earlier years of schooling, to use some manipulative and authoritarian methods in order to ensure the success of later, more high-level teaching strategies.[4] Informed critique, for example, builds on accurate factual recall as well as analytic capacity.

The content criterion does not, at first, appear to pose problems for the POSITIVIST model. No bias toward a particular kind of content is necessarily implied by adoption of the model. Nevertheless, it is historically the case that teachers who lean toward "the scientific method in education" have often tended to scorn those subjects which lack the apparent solidity and certainty of scientific fact, and it is undoubtedly true that behavioral objectives are easier to write for the learning of facts and skills than

---

[4]John Wilson, "Indoctrination and Rationality" in *Concepts of Indoctrination*, ed. I. A. Snook (London: Routledge & Kegan Paul, 1972), p. 17.

for the higher-order processes of reasoning, appreciating, and valuing.

As for intention and outcome, it is probable that teaching on the POSITIVIST model not only would appeal to those who *wanted* to indoctrinate, but would tend to produce effects of indoctrination despite teachers of good will. Those who control society tend to control the curriculum and to enforce the status quo. The teacher's own stance would also influence the determination of lesson content, but the requirements of successful behavioral programming would prevent students from calling into question the implicit rationale of the programming. In short, here is a model to be used sparingly if we wish to minimize the likelihood of indoctrination.

The RATIONALIST model appears to fare very well in this assessment. It seeks pre-eminently to encourage critical rationality, the appraisal of evidence, the attitude of knowing what you believe and why you believe it. A practical problem arises from the fact that it depends for its success on the student's having reached the stage at which he *can* think for himself and handle abstract concepts. This reduces the applicability of the model in the earlier years of schooling, and reminds us that it is not a self-sufficient approach to teaching.

The commitment to critical rationality which underlies the model does not render it neutral and thus impervious to the charge of indoctrination. The teacher who claims she is sustaining in the classroom a climate of open discussion and impartial inquiry may be doing so either as a means toward helping statements to enter into examined commitments of their own, or as an exercise in intellectual dilettantism which encourages students to adopt a life-stance of detachment and fence-sitting—an unwillingness to commit themselves to persons and causes, or to take the plunge on the big questions about the meaning and purpose of life. Not only is it important to test the motives of the teacher who adopts this model, but it is also relevant to query the unintended effects of the procedures adopted. A love of debate and a lack of compassion is no neutral outcome, and if this has been fostered, intentionally or inadvertently, by the teacher's stance, itself unexamined in class, then indoctrination will to some extent have occurred.

The PERSONALIST model appears to promise good things

112   because it enshrines an intention to foster personal growth and self-awareness in an environment allegedly the very opposite of authoritarian. But this view neglects the inevitability of the teacher's having to take a stand on the ground rules applying to the personal interactions of the classroom. There is no one answer to which rules are the best. Some teachers tend to a strong paternalism ("I know best"), others to indulgent permissiveness ("Do what you want"). This variability will extend to both the aims the teacher has in mind for the pupil, and the methods he chooses to achieve these aims.

No one will question that the teacher desires to lead the pupil toward self-realization, empathy, and respect for persons. This puts needed flesh on the bones of the RATIONALIST model. But do the teacher's intentions stop short of molding the pupil in the teacher's own image? The ambiguous possibilities inherent in the model stem from the potential effects of a strong teacher-pupil relationship, which serves to inhibit the student from critically reviewing the teacher's own stance.

EDUCATION

So far I have been concerned with asking where each of the three teaching models stands with respect to the concept of indoctrination, but this question will only be bothersome to those who favor a particular concept of education stressing the development of rational and responsible individuals. For them, indoctrination is a term of disapproval which is the very opposite of education. In a book of studies analyzing the concept of indoctrination, R. H. Gatchel's description of how the two concepts have evolved associates *this* concept of education with liberal democratic ideology, thereby implying that those who do *not* give "education" this value-loading may not necessarily perceive indoctrination as miseducative.[5]

At this point it is useful to ask where Christians stand in the debate. There can be no doubt that some Christians worry very little about the things they do to individuals, invading their privacy and integrity, so long as the result is a profession of faith in Christ. From the evangelism by physical torture of some previous centuries to the evangelism by psychological manipulation of many present-day Christians, the end has been held to justify the means.

[5]R. H. Gatchel, "The Evolution of the Concept" in *Concepts of Indoctrination*, ed. I. A. Snook (London: Routledge & Kegan Paul, 1972), p. 13.

But if the end is not a person who responds to God freely and 113
responsibly at all levels of her personality, then Scriptural conditions have not been fulfilled. As we saw in Chapter One, Jesus
pushed inquirers to clearly understand what they were doing before they joined forces with him.

In cases in which manipulation outweighs the appeal to reason,
zeal for souls leads to a heavily paternalistic version of the PER-
SONALIST model of teaching, with a liberal use of the POSI-
TIVIST model in its most deterministic form, combining to
minimize that thinking part of personality which is one of the
primary attributes of the image of God in us. Does this mean,
then, that as Christians we should favor the RATIONALIST
model? This model has been much advocated in recent discussions
of the concept of education, especially as analyzed by R. S. Peters
in London and others of the same mind, including such confirmed
humanists as R. F. Dearden. In a famous and technically skilled
analysis of the concept of education that is now widely reflected
in ordinary usage, Peters originally claimed that the term "education" picked out a family of activities aimed at developing
knowledge and understanding in the learner. Building on this,
Dearden argued for special emphasis on rational autonomy and
critical thinking.[6] It subsequently became clear, among the philosophical fraternity who were testing Peters' claim, that he was
not simply describing what users of ordinary language mean by
"education" but tightening up the concept to reflect a value judgment, admittedly popular in "educational circles," that man is at
his best when he is most rational, and schooling should be directed at developing this side of his nature.

One can see motivations of this kind underlying preference for
the RATIONALIST model of teaching, but it is proper to suggest
that there is a fuller concept of education also abroad in educational
circles which is more PERSONALIST but does not deny that
reason is *one* of the attributes to be enhanced. This concept sup-
plements the development of critical awareness with the nurture

[6]The point is reiterated by R. S. Peters and P. H. Hirst in their widely used
book for students of the philosophy of education entitled *The Logic of Education*
(London: Routledge & Kegan Paul, 1970), p. 24. See also R. F. Dearden, "Autonomy and Education" in *Education and the Development of Reason*, ed. R. F.
Dearden, P. H. Hirst, and R. S. Peters (London: Routledge & Kegan Paul,
1972), pp. 440–466.

of good will toward other persons and a willingness to commit oneself to the feelings and relationships proven, by personal experience as well as by rational reflection, to be enriching and mutual.

Peters rests his case by appealing to the widespread use of the RATIONALIST model in educational circles. I believe I can do the same in regard to this more PERSONALIST concept, which is much in evidence in current free-school literature and in debates about "open education," and has always been a part of educational theories built on Judeo–Christian assumptions. Our job must now be to bring the two streams together. A starting point could well be Englishman M. V. C. Jeffrey's emphasis on persons as rational *and moral* beings, in whose education the deepening of feeling is as important as the sharpening of thinking.[7] There was also Philip Phenix's criticism, offered in 1964, that the current conception of rationality tended to exclude "the life of feeling, conscience, imagination, and other processes that are not rational in the strict sense."[8]

I have tried to show that both the Scriptures and current educational theorizing encourage us to support a view of schooling which emphasizes the development of persons who combine knowledge and critical thinking with sensitivity and a commitment to the good of others. We seek not docile conformists but compassionate autonomists. On the assumption that this view is acceptable, I now affirm the possibility of spelling out clear guidelines concerning the teacher's expressing her own personal beliefs in the classroom. I will identify in turn four possibilities, and discuss their suitability from an ethical and practical point of view.

EXCLUSIVE PARTIALITY

A stance of "exclusive partiality" represents a decision on the part of the teacher (and perhaps on the part of the school authorities) to impart his personal and religious beliefs in a manner which

[7]M. V. C. Jeffreys, *Personal Values and the Modern World* (New York: Penguin Books, 1962).

[8]Philip H. Phenix, *Realms of Meaning* (New York: McGraw-Hill, 1964), p. 21. I cite Jeffreys and Phenix as Christians working as professors of education in the secular world. They contrast sharply with Christian theorists who write only to be read by Christians.

precludes challenge. The logic of this stance is that if there are things which I believe to be true, then, regardless of the fact that in my pluralistic society there are many thoughtful and intelligent people who have different views, I am justified in teaching my beliefs as true, and ignoring dissenting opinions. We should be warned that this policy, which is followed in some Christian schools, is also adopted in Communist countries and many Islamic schools. Are our valuations of human personality as similar as that?

In view of what has already been said, the Christian response is to affirm that individuals need to be made aware of the kind of world they inhabit and the options which invite their allegiance, so that their choice of Christ may be sufficiently thought through to enable them to stand against the persuasions of alternative faiths. Cocooned Christians are just the ones likely to be led astray by those the Scriptures call "false teachers," who make their appeal to the "itching ears" of the immature.[9]

Where a policy of exclusive partiality is adopted in the interests of Christian truth, the result is a heavily paternalistic version of the PERSONALIST model of teaching. Where the school or teacher is antagonistic to this religious perspective—as in, say, the scientific behaviorism of B. F. Skinner[10]—the result is an Orwellian exploitation of the POSITIVIST model.

EXCLUSIVE NEUTRALITY

At the other end of the continuum is the stance of "exclusive neutrality," which represents a decision to keep such controversial areas of study as religion and politics out of the curriculum altogether. This policy obliges the teacher to prevent discussion in the classroom, as well as representation in the syllabus to be taught, of any beliefs and values which are objects of heated debate in the community at large, or else simply of any opinions which have not been empirically verified. Much has been said about the need to keep public education systems neutral in this sense. In my own country of Australia, state systems of education

[9]See, for example, II Timothy 3 and 4.
[10]See especially his *Science and Human Behavior* (New York: Free Press and Collier-Macmillan, 1953), and other citations in footnote 15 of Chapter Two.

have followed this injunction so faithfully that the result is a bleached, fact-loaded academic curriculum, even though some states provide for a nominal and unexaminable period of religious instruction. In the U.S., the impossibility of neutrality has been driven home by the spectacle of a public education which ostentatiously bars religious studies and by default promotes a vague kind of secular humanism which is the more pernicious for being unadmitted and therefore unexamined by the students at the level of presuppositions.

Several arguments show that this stance is as untenable as it is undesirable. The very fact that the areas of study excluded are matters of controversy in the community at large says something about their importance in the environment we are trying to help our students come to terms with. The teacher's silence has the indoctrinative effect of implying that such issues don't really matter in working out one's life priorities. It is also arguable that the policy encourages the deepening of rifts between different ideological groups in the community, because no encouragement is given to the rational practice of "talking things over." In Chapter Three it was also argued that the exclusion of religion distorts the curriculum balance.

NEUTRAL IMPARTIALITY

Answering the criticisms of the previous stance, many recent curriculum projects have provided for the inclusion of descriptive material in areas of controversy, and in some cases have advocated the practice of rational inspection and discussion. Many have viewed the technique of "values clarification" as a move in this direction, but it is evident that the object here is to help students clarify the values that animate them, but not to critique those which animate others. The implication is that values are personal and subjective, not subject to rational defense or negotiation. This is not a neutral assumption, but a vote in favor of relativism. Other strategies go further in inviting discussion and analysis, but the distinguishing feature of this stance is that the teacher must remain neutral in the sense that he does not reveal his own personal stance. He conceals it to avoid exerting undue psychological pressure on the students, or implying that the school system has a stance in such matters.

As one might expect, those drawn to the PERSONALIST   *117*
model find this limitation distasteful because it falsifies the teacher's
relationship with students and distorts his testimony to his own
personal being. One writer has described the teacher as one who
not only imparts truths and skills by instruction but *is*, in his
person, "a truth for students."[11] In making this point, the writer
was not speaking for Christians, but for that broad movement of
thought called existentialism. But it is, of course, the kind of
point a Christian is bound to make. The educative impact of
personal witness and lifestyle is constantly driven home in the
Scriptures.

To require the teacher to conceal her own personal beliefs at
those points at which they might be regarded as relevant inputs
to the lesson (points at which children were being invited to
express their personal views, anyway) sets at risk our declared
curriculum objectives. How is one to interpret the teacher's coy
restraint? As Mary Warnock has observed, "It is hard for pupils,
especially if they are quite young, to realize that the neutral teacher
is only play-acting."[12]

One interpretation which follows from such conduct is that it
is better to be a fence-sitter than someone who admits to having
beliefs that are not finally provable (because they are of an all-
embracing kind, and empirical proof applies only to individual
phenomena) but are considered to be reasonable. Another is that
beliefs of this kind should not be exposed to rational examination
or their psychological power to animate conduct will fade. One
might reply that the stance of neutral impartiality can very well
encourage rational critique, but if the teacher declines to take a
stand on some issue, or to let his stand be analyzed, despite having
encouraged students to reveal where they stand and to discuss the
issues raised, then the genuineness of his advocacy of rational
discourse itself is called into question.

The stance of neutral impartiality may be criticized on another
ground, namely, that it can never finally be successfully implemented. No person in daily contact with others can avoid revealing something of the beliefs and values which motivate his

[11]G. S. Belkin, "The Teacher as Hero," *Educational Theory*, 22 (Spring 1972),
419.
[12]Mary Warnock, "The Neutral Teacher" in *Philosophers Discuss Education*,
ed. S. C. Brown (London: Macmillan, 1975), p. 170.

behavior. Though he may resolve to say nothing directly about his convictions, random comments and non-verbal cues build a picture in the minds of his associates. Question any school children about their teachers, and much will emerge which the subjects under scrutiny did not know they were revealing. Since, however, this data has been gathered under conditions of hidden appraisal, it can have bad outcomes. Students may choose to copy some of the teacher's more idiosyncratic behavior without understanding the motivations and convictions which led him to act this way. They may make wrong inferences about the teacher's beliefs, and experience uneasiness because they cannot clearly see what role beliefs play in behavior.

Neutral impartiality favors most the RATIONALIST model of teaching, though we have seen that it may distort the understanding children have of the role of rationality in commitment. It places more severe limits on those who lean toward the PERSONALIST model. And it renders the Christian teacher powerless at the very point at which he can potentially be most helpful to his students.

COMMITTED IMPARTIALITY

The fourth stance accepts all that the third stance has to offer, but also legitimates the teacher's revealing her personal beliefs at relevant points in classroom interaction. In terms of ethical guidelines, this stance may be spelled out in two complementary rules. One is that the teacher should foster the critical analysis and inspection of alternative viewpoints on matters of important and controversial belief. That satisfies the requirements of the RATIONALIST model. The second rule is that the teacher should allow herself to be seen as a person embracing commitments for what she deems to be good reasons, provided that she preserves impartiality in her treatment of students. This fulfills the requirements of the PERSONALIST model, but with ethical safeguards against exerting undue pressure at a personal level.

The model of humanness underlying this policy is that of a person who values rationality, and uses it continuously to refine his beliefs and attitudes and bring them closer to what he believes to be the true nature of reality and the meaning of life. He is also one who feels committed to the welfare of persons, an individual willing to get involved and to participate in a morally responsible way in the interpersonal world. The natural man who tends toward this model is, in the words of Jesus to the insightful scribe, "not far from the kingdom of God" (Mark 13:34); he is a person ripe to hear the momentous invitation, "Follow me."

All this is heady stuff, but the skeptic will want to point out that the recommended stance is not practicable. That very power of the teacher to influence children will tip the scales toward indoctrination if given the free rein implied by the second guideline. But the guideline is not unrestricted. It calls for the self-control necessary to treat all children alike and to avoid playing favorites. If those who urge neutral impartiality are doing so in order to avoid these difficulties, then not only do they produce a different crop of difficulties (as previously discussed), but they skirt the duty of helping the teacher to make it work. As Kleinig has said, if the reason for advocating what I have called neutral impartiality is fear of "the excessive authority which the teacher's word possesses," then the solution lies not in the adoption of such a dubious alternative but in a study of "those features of the teaching situation, the teacher's methods, and the cultural background, which give rise to such excess."[13]

Further, where the school adopts either policy of neutrality outlined above, the people set at the greatest disadvantage are those who are the most ethical and morally serious. They will feel obliged to honor the contract under which they operate. Increasingly, however, people of less firm moral fiber are taking the opportunity which the classroom affords them to pressure their students to adopt markedly deviant values which are not submitted to rational critique and comparison and are not agreeable to the parents responsible for those students in their dependent years. In practical terms (as distinct from the logical considerations we noted earlier), neutral policies are not working for this reason.

Hence, despite the acknowledged difficulties of implementing a policy of committed impartiality, we must work at it and increase the acceptance and understanding of it by teachers, administrators, and parents.

In one particular respect this discussion has significant impli-

[13]Kleinig, "Mill, Children, and Rights," p. 15.

cations for the teacher in a Christian school as well. It suggests that, regardless of the generally closer value-agreement in such a school, the teacher should not capitalize on this opportunity to veer toward the stance of exclusive partiality. Not only is it good education to help students to weigh alternative points of view, but it is honoring to God to help them become as responsible as they may for the decisions they make and the beliefs they decide to adopt. In a compulsory classroom setting, we must be highly sensitive to the integrity of our students, and not pressure them to conform to a Christian behavior pattern or to mouth beliefs they may not personally hold.

Two further criteria need to be mentioned in spelling out the implications of our guidelines for committed impartiality. One is empirical, and relates to the developmental stages through which children pass. Both in promoting rational critique and in displaying his own beliefs, the teacher should be sensitive to the capacity of children to handle these experiences. Cognitive development moves through several stages before children reach the point at which they can comfortably handle general ideas. Emotionally they move from strong dependency on authority figures to greater self-dependency. Each factor may at times oblige the teacher to draw back for the time being.

The second is logical, and relates to the criterion of relevance. The teacher who has the opportunity to reveal his own beliefs should not take this as an open invitation to pour out his soul whenever openings arise in classroom interchange. The question should be; "Will my entry into this discussion as a committed person contribute to the educational objectives (not the evangelistic objectives) of my lesson? And what is it relevant for me to say?" One practical guideline may help you to answer this question: wait until *the students* ask you for your opinion, and then answer *their* question specifically, honestly, *and briefly*. You will not need to say much to prove that you are a committed person. Say too much, and you will find it harder to function as the arbitrator and umpire of the classroom discussion.

POSTSCRIPT

The ideal set forth in this chapter is not widely held by the public or by teachers and administrators in public or (for different reasons) private schools. The Christian teacher cannot simply begin to implement the guidelines overnight. Some teachers, habituated to a policy of neutrality, will find it threatening; many parents will want reassurances that it does not open the door to prose-lytization in the classroom. Adoption of such a policy in a school or school system must be the result of open discussion and agree-ment—not everyone will be won over in a day. The main thrust of this chapter is to help Christian teachers come to a reasoned belief about what, ideally, their stance should be. Too many dis-cussions lack point because the participants are not clear about the positions they are arguing *from*.

Compromises may have to be negotiated. In particular, those teachers who are averse to exposing their own convictions on such matters as religion may need to be offered the option of retaining the stance of neutral impartiality. That is considerably better than nothing. Conversely, teachers who embrace commit-ted impartiality should not be unwilling to reveal to parents and administrators any views they are prepared to share with their students. Such implications will need to be explored. I hope I have shown, however, that there is a position which Christian teachers may adopt with confidence that it is good educational practice, and with equal confidence that it is consistent with the example set in the Scriptures by our Lord.

7 Teaching Style

"What should my style be as a professional teacher?"

WE have thought about the ethics of compulsory education and of revealing our own personal beliefs in the classroom. We have considered some of the questions of knowledge and curriculum content, including the case for catering to religious studies in our subject matter. We have pondered the relationship between home and school, and asked whether this implies the setting up of Christian schools or more community involvement in public schools. Through it all we have attempted to apply a Christian mind to questions of our professional practice as teachers. But, ethics and expertise aside, what sort of people will we be when we "get it all together"? What makes a good Christian teacher in the round? Times have changed a great deal since an English village in the last century laid down the duties of the schoolmaster in the following terms:

1. To teach all standards.
2. To sweep and clean the school.
3. To ring the church bell on Sunday.
4. To dig all graves.
[And etc.!]

Those in the teaching profession, and, I suspect, Christian teachers, are today confused about what is an appropriate professional style. Should the teacher be authoritative or permissive? Should she instruct or counsel? Should she display her professional expertise or play it down to encourage community involvement?

This chapter is adapted from an article entitled "Teaching as Reconciliation" in the Journal of Christian Education, *Papers 56, Dec. 1976, pp. 8-16.*

Should the pupil be encouraged to see his teacher as scholar, or friend, or magistrate, or stagehand?

Other occupations have their accepted images. Dentists and plumbers have recognizable styles (and have some things in common!). Bus conductors have few qualms about how they ought to behave. But teachers not only have to live down the literary legacy of schoolmasters in the mold of Mr. Chips and Mr. Squeers, but also cope with the contradictory expectations of a pluralistic society, which range from impersonal professional technique to totally egalitarian subjectivity. What image shall guide us?

Partial answers can be found by analyzing meanings in ordinary language, surveying social expectations, and empirically studying acts of teaching and teaching skills. But there is no guarantee that these will add up to a unified view of what makes a good teacher. There remains a question of style, which is ultimately a personal matter, and dependent on one's own view of oneself and other persons. Teaching involves the attempt by some persons to guide the learning of others. Acquiring an arsenal of teaching skills and competencies merely improves our ability to get the result we are after. The question still to be asked is, What result *should* we want, as teachers? The answer does not merely give us our general aims but affects our daily teaching procedures. As R. S. Peters once pointed out, our fundamental goals are mere icing on the cake unless they implicate our everyday strategies of classroom management and instruction.[1]

We are, then, to borrow the words of a recent book title, "in search of a teaching style."[2] It is unlikely that this quest will produce a single answer, for even if reasonable agreement is reached on a professional ethic and a professional empiric, there will remain a personal factor, because style has aesthetic elements as well. Framing the question a different way, then, Is there anything that the Christian teacher can glean from the Scriptures to help her in developing an appropriate professional style?

Of course there is. The Scriptures teem with precepts and illustrations which throw the teaching role into sharper relief. I

[1]R. S. Peters, *Authority, Responsibility and Education* (London: George Allen & Unwin, 1959), p. 96.

[2]Abraham Shumsky, *In Search of a Teaching Style* (New York: Appleton-Century, 1968).

124   propose to pick out just one idea which helps me to conceptualize
my role in a Christian way. It is the idea of reconciliation.

THE CONCEPT OF RECONCILIATION

The word "reconciliation" immediately summons to the Christian mind the words of II Corinthians 5:18-20:

> All this is from God, who reconciled us to himself through
> Christ and gave us the ministry of reconciliation; that God
> was reconciling the world to himself in Christ, not counting
> man's sins against them. And he has committed to us the
> message of reconciliation. We are therefore Christ's
> ambassadors.

The notion of reconciliation presented here applies in the first
place to direct evangelism, but it is not inappropriate (as I shall
argue later) to apply it to our professional behavior.

We must begin by giving the word its full biblical weight. In
current English, "reconciliation" can refer merely to two estranged persons deciding to bury the hatchet and be friends again.
But in Scripture it has the additional dimension of enmity between the two parties because one party—man—has deeply
wronged the other, innocent party—God.[3] It is a term which
probes beyond the occasional disagreements that occur between
people to a fundamental flaw in the world order caused by our
race's rebellion against God. In this situation, it is not just a matter
of our being reconciled to God when it pleases us. It is for God
to reconcile *us* to himself. The initiative lies with him, and it has
been a costly one.

The second biblical implication is that reconciliation cannot be
effective without both the knowledge and the consent of the parties involved. I must *know* the true state of affairs, and I must
consent to be reconciled to God. It is not something that happens
while I'm asleep.

Hence, "reconciliation" in the Christian sense grapples with
things that are seriously out of joint. This calls for a stern realism

---

[3]See "Reconciliation" in the *New Bible Dictionary* (London: InterVarsity Press,
1962); and Chapter Six in Leon Morris, *The Apostolic Preaching of the Cross*
(London: Tyndale Press, 1955).

in dealing with the facts of the present world order and the visions people have for human betterment, especially through education.

How, then, is the general ministry of reconciliation applicable to the professional style of a Christian teacher? I will discuss three points at which it has particular relevance: (1) in reconciling the child to society; (2) in reconciling the education of thinking and the education of feeling; and (3) in reconciling the various agents involved in providing education.

CHILD AND SOCIETY

It may seem odd to speak of a need to reconcile the child to society. Surely the child is already a product of society, needing only to be made more aware of his position in the social matrix so that he can become a well-adjusted and contributing member. But the problem with this view is that it slips so easily into servile contentment with the status quo. And the status quo is *always* morally deficient. There is enmity in existing social structures which requires prophetic exposure. This is why, for example, we *must* bring moral judgments into our social studies.

Alternatively, it is said that the resources for social improvement lie within the individual, who is to be allowed to develop in his own way, along the lines of his own intrinsic curiosity and interest. This, we are assured, will bring into being a race of naturally altruistic humanists, who will reconstruct the faulty structures of society. But the problem with this view is that it ignores both the complexity of the power structures in a technological society and the tendencies to self-assertion and egoism in the human personality.

The Christian teacher is obliged to alert the learner to the enmities as well as the excellencies of man, both in history and in literature, because a prerequisite of reconciliation is that the parties be *aware* of their need to be reconciled. Similarly, the Christian teacher's discipline in class will be reconciliatory. He will not permit disruptive behavior in the name of a romantic philosophy of freedom. But neither will he deem it sufficient merely to subdue those who offend. Rather, he will seek the opportunity to bring them to terms with themselves and with the external forces that goad them.

In the teaching service today there is a tendency to polarize

126   people into two groups: those who come down hard on the side
       of strict classroom control and direct teaching, and those who
       deny that children should be compelled to do anything. The first
       group ignores the enmity inherent in all human authority struc-
       tures. The second denies the perversity which surfaces in indi-
       viduals when social restraints are abolished. The Christian teacher
       is in a good position to mediate between these extremes, putting
       himself and the child on guard against perfectionist views of either
       society or the individual.

THE EDUCATION OF THINKING AND FEELING

The second plane of reconciliation is between the education of
thinking and the education of feeling. Once again, one's natural
reaction in the present climate of thought is to say, "Why talk of
reconciliation in this connection? Why don't you simply say that
we should pay attention to both aspects in order to get a balanced
education?"

But I persist with the metaphor of reconciliation because I
perceive a quarrel of strangely major dimensions between those
who stress cognitive and rational objectives on the one hand, and
those who stress effective and interpersonal objectives on the
other. This issue was investigated in Chapter Two. There we saw
that proponents in each camp tend to speak scathingly of each
other, as when Peters deplores the "mystic confrontations" which
Martin Buber expounds,[4] and the followers of Carl Rogers decline, as he did, to prescribe in advance any necessary cognitive
content for pupils. It really seems peculiarly difficult to get the
theorists to agree on what constitutes a desirable balance.

This is so because, at root, we are seeing a battle between
ideologies, between rival theories of man. The stoutest defenders
of rationality and cognitive transformation are old-style humanists, confident in the reasonableness of man. The stoutest defenders of truth through our feelings and personal relationships are
the "new humanists" who have resurrected Rousseau's belief in
the innate goodness of man's spontaneous self.

One frequently encounters college students, sublimely indif-
ferent to the history of ideas but familiar with Carl Rogers, who

---

[4]R. S. Peters, *Ethics and Education,* esp. Chapter 2.

begin their essays by saying that they believe that the child is naturally wise and good. The distressing thing is not the fact that they have such a belief, for we all work from presuppositions, but that they do not accept the need to submit this belief to analysis or criticism. They are estranged from rational discourse.

Why is this cleavage in educational theory so deep? May it not be symptomatic of the enmity at the heart of the human personality which drives a wedge between knowing the right and desiring it, and between wanting the good and doing it? Plato pictures reason as the charioteer drawing the reins on those two spirited steeds, the will and the appetites, but it would be more accurate to depict three steeds trying to get into a vacant chariot while the divine charioteer waits to be acknowledged. Man is at enmity within himself.

The teacher's task as reconciler is complicated. He must encourage children to use and cherish reason without forgetting its limits. He must commend the use of intelligence but avoid giving preferential treatment to the most intelligent. He must foster sensitivity and warm relationships without forcing the behavioral stereotypes of his own social class onto children coming from backgrounds different from his own. He must be a person at peace with himself, head and heart bridled by a higher agency.

Even if the teacher meets all these conditions (and who has the capacity to do so?), a unified and cooperative classroom cannot be guaranteed. The path of the reconciler, as we shall see in a moment, is strewn with hardships. Nevertheless, that teacher will be memorable, a continuing recommendation to his former students of the greater reconciling friendship with God.

THE AGENTS OF EDUCATION

The third area of reconciliation is that of educational decision-making, at the point where the various interested parties in education encounter each other in the making of curriculum policies. And what a battlefield it is! Teachers' unions lock horns with school boards; both parental expressions of concern and parental apathy alike prompt teachers to close ranks and resist community involvement; mutual resentment exists between many school administrators and their teaching staff; outside groups encourage senior students to create a revolutionary situation in the schools.

The answer to these pressures does not merely lie, as some would have us think, in dismantling the educational bureaucracy and moving to radically de-institutionalized forms of educational resource. Community schools and learning resource centers are themselves constantly sub-dividing, as the individualists who first led the breakaway from traditional forms experience fallings-out among themselves.

We are reaping the fruits of what C. S. Lewis has called the "unchristening of the west"—the fragmentation of human groups due not to the anonymity of the suburban lifestyle but to the self-centered materialism which has been our first step back into paganism. The signs of enmity are everywhere. Disruption is preferred to conciliation; confrontation to negotiation. Revolution or desertion has much more appeal than arduous piecemeal reform.

Often the critics and agitators speak the truth. Our school systems *are* in a mess, and our training schedules are in disarray. But they speak the truth in enmity, excluding the possibility that the interested parties might actually be able to come and reason together. The Christian reconciler is charged to speak the truth *in love* (Eph. 4:15), which means that he must never lose sight of the fact that he is dealing with people. He will stick to the issues, resisting the temptation to indulge in name-calling and to describe the problems in terms of class warfare, or in terms of Christian versus non-believer. Fallible mortals are on *both* sides of every schism.

An example of a reconciler at work came to my attention in an Illinois church some years ago, when a teacher's strike was arousing great bitterness even between Christians, who were on both sides of the issue. The pastor chose to make a statement, which included the following observation:

> I want to say something about the strike in Unit 4 schools. For many of you this is a painful time. . . . You're not all on the same side. . . . But a great many of you are alike in one way: you are worried and upset, you are losing sleep at night, and you're terribly concerned.
>
> You're alike in another way: you are Christians. And it's very important just now that you remember the things that Christians know . . . We know about sin. . . . All of us have sinned. . . . [So] we mustn't expect too much of one another. Now some very unfortunate things have been said

and done, and as emotions rise that's going to be even more
true. I'm saying that we must be willing to accept that, and
quick to forgive; and not demand that people under great
pressure act like angels, because they're not.

Here one sees a reconciler at work. He expects his people to be
fighting for principles, but he urges them to be alert to heal, to
bind up wounds, and to seek the truth in love.

BUT IS THIS THE BIBLICAL MINISTRY OF
RECONCILIATION?

Here, then, are three areas in which the notion of reconciliation
has an impact on the teacher's professional style. But the earlier
question must be faced. The Bible passage I quoted from was not
talking about classroom and staff-room behavior, but something
else:

> We are therefore Christ's ambassadors, as though God were
> making his appeal through us. We implore you on Christ's
> behalf: Be reconciled to God. (II Cor. 5:20)

The emphasis here is on reconciling men and women *to God*, not
to society or to themselves. The Christian's primary mission is
evangelism, and it is in evangelism that the biblical notion of
reconciliation is imbedded. Indeed, say some, stretching the word
to make it apply to social action in general can only lead to a
dilution of the gospel imperative.

I disagree with this point of view, which I shall describe as
"fundamentalist." Evangelical Christianity responds to the whole,
balanced word of Scripture, and there are many biblical grounds
for regarding this view as a restricted perception of our mission.
For now, it is enough to read the verses in context by going back
to verses 3-6 in II Corinthians 6:

> We put no stumbling block in anyone's path, so that our
> ministry will not be discredited. Rather, as servants of God
> we commend ourselves in every way: in great endurance;
> in troubles, hardships and distresses; in beatings, impris-
> onments and riots; in hard work, sleepless nights and hun-
> ger; in purity, understanding, patience and kindness. . . .

And so on. In short, while evangelism is assuredly what we as

130   Christians have primarily in mind, it is inseparable from the more mundane details of our daily walk, including our professional vocation. This is a linkage which, I suggest, is to be maintained in three ways.

OUR GENERAL WITNESS MAKES OR MARS OUR SPECIAL TESTIMONY

The first thing the passage teaches is that our general witness, including our professional style, makes or mars our evangelistic efforts. Who has not met the teacher active in the church who neglects to keep her lesson preparation and marking up-to-date because of her many church commitments? Or the strict and sour principal who preaches on Sunday about the love of God? To interpret the passage at its lowest level of meaning, we must do our secular job with all our might in order that our gospel may not be discredited.

At a higher level, the passage speaks not merely of a match between message and lifestyle, but of the inevitability of suffering. If we are truly involved, living and laboring alongside the people we desire to evangelize, we'll get bruised. Flogging and imprisonment may not be the lot of teachers, but overwork and lack of sleep surely are! That is the price of reconciliation, from the stable to the staff room.

But this very immersion of our selves in the life-stream of our neighbors at home and in the school enhances our gospel in a still more profound way. For only in this way can we discover at what points the gospel will strike home, what the needs are of the people to whom we are presenting Christ. We must remember how irrelevant many of our organized church campaigns are to the ongoing concerns and needs of the unchurched.

THE GOSPEL ENRICHES OUR GENERAL WITNESS

The other side of the coin is that our general witness is enlightened and deepened by the gospel in which we believe. If, for example, we have been entrusted with the central message of reconciliation—of how men and women may get right with God—then the ministry of reconciliation spills over into all areas of life.

When we encounter abused and disadvantaged children, we recommend our message by our patience and kindliness. When we are derided in the staff room or at the parent-teacher meeting, we recommend our message by refusing to give offense and by continuing to speak the truth. When we encounter lies or bullying in the government or the union, we recommend our message by the innocence of our behavior and our grasp of the truth about people.

We have the freedom to crusade against enmities in our classroom and in the larger spheres of our involvement because the most deep-rooted enmity of all has been eradicated from our hearts. Being reconciled with God, we yearn to see the yeast of reconciliation spreading through our beleaguered world, beginning in our school. It is in this sense that the gospel enriches our general witness.

INVOLVEMENT IS ESSENTIAL

Third, drawing the threads together, the Christian lifestyle is not fence-sitting while the world feuds, but involvement at every point. Nor is it enough to make sporadic contact with the world for evangelistic purposes. Evangelical Christians in the present century have been too unconcerned about the social setting in which they proclaim their gospel, although the recent Lausanne declaration of social concern is a hopeful sign that this imbalance is beginning to be corrected. The teaching profession must not lag behind in the response.

Too many well-intentioned Christian teachers and teacher educators have confined their professional testimony to good teaching and a warm concern for their students as individuals, building comely structures while bigger tides of social change have crept up on their work. Few have felt called to be activists in the academic, political, and industrial aspects of their profession as well, and curricular change has proceeded rapidly, often without the leavening influence of Christian expertise. It may be that part of the reason for such neglect has been not only a defective view of how the gospel of reconciliation is to be communicated, but a very human fear of getting hurt.

For Christian witness is punishing work. Reconciliation is a costly lifestyle, as later verses in our passage (II Cor. 6:8-10) make clear:

> Through glory and dishonor, bad report and good report; genuine, yet regarded as impostors; known, yet regarded as unknown . . . poor, yet making many rich; having nothing, and yet possessing everything. . . .

We submit to the labels people pin on us—fanatic, scab, killjoy, puritan—not just because of the gospel message we proclaim, but because we won't fight dirty, we won't write off any child, we won't endorse political polarizations into "us" and "them"—not even when we find ourselves, for conscience' sake, pilloried by a whole staff room.

And yet . . . and yet . . . from time to time, individuals who joined in the general sneering seek us out to ask why we act the way we do, and we see in their query an implicit cry to be rid of the enmity which is corroding their spirits. Involvement has its price, but it also has its rewards, its causes for joy.

Conclusion

THE whole of this book has been an exercise in involvement, an attempt to address a number of philosophical questions which concern not only Christian teachers but all who are engaged in the profession of teaching. I have attempted to explore these issues not from behind the ramparts of theological affirmations which will be acceptable only to my in-group, but by appeal to arguments that may carry weight in the open arena of consultation and planning by the interested parties involved in our schools, especially in the public sector.

I have also attempted to help the Christian teacher serving in the public sector to think his way through to a Christian rationale for the job he is doing, for too often Christian theorists have implied that he is something of a second-class citizen compared to the teacher serving in a Christian school. On the contrary, it is possible that he is often somewhat nearer to the front line. But all Christian teachers, wherever they are presently carrying out their professional functions, are of the utmost strategic importance to the advancement of God's kingdom, and need to clearly understand how their job meshes with their faith.

In the introductory chapter I developed a diagram showing the many areas which need to be brought under the scrutiny of Christian minds, and I admitted that the present book had merely sampled a few of them. I find it exciting that there is so much scope here for vigorous and original Christian thought, and I would like to think that readers of this book will take up the task of thinking Christianly about many of these areas and sharing their findings with the rest of us. In the introductory chapter I also spoke of the body of Christians in the teaching profession as a sleeping giant. In these uncertain times it is appropriate to call out in the words of Paul found in Ephesians 3:14:

> Wake up, O sleeper,
> rise from the dead,
> and Christ will shine upon you.

Selected Bibliography

Australian Teachers' Christian Fellowship, Teacher Action Study Kits (TASKs), Sydney, Australia: ATCF Books, as listed:

Because I Say So! Thinking Christianly About Classroom Discipline and Punishment, 1978.

First Year Out: Thinking Christianly About the Induction of New Teachers, 1980.

In Other Words: Thinking Christianly About English Language in the Curriculum, 1980.

School for Parents? Thinking Christianly About Community Involvement in Schools, 1979.

Servants or Subversives? Thinking Christianly About the Christian Presence in the School, 1981.

Teachers of Sound Mind: Thinking Christianly About the Mental Health of Teachers, 1979.

Teaching Evolution: Thinking Christianly About the Teaching of Human Origins, 1982.

Time for Religion: Thinking Christianly About Religious Studies in School, 1982.

Beck, C. M., et al., eds. *Moral Education: Interdisciplinary Approaches.* Toronto: University of Toronto Press, 1971.

Bereiter, Carl. *Must We Educate?* Englewood Cliffs, N.J.: Prentice-Hall, 1975.

Blamires, Harry. *The Christian Mind.* London: S.P.C.K., 1963.

Blishen, Edward, ed. *The School That I'd Like.* New York: Penguin Books, 1969.

Brown, S. C., ed. *Philosophers Discuss Education.* London: Macmillan, 1975.

Buber, Martin. *I and Thou.* Trans. Ronald Gregor Smith. 2nd ed. New York: Charles Scribner's Sons, 1958.

————. *The Knowledge of Man.* Trans. Maurice Friedman and Ronald Gregor Smith. London: George Allen & Unwin, 1965.

————. *Paths in Utopia.* Trans. R. F. C. Hull. London: Routledge & Kegan Paul, 1949.

136   D'Cruz, J. V., and P. J. Sheehan, eds. *Concepts in Education*. Melbourne, Australia: Dove Publications, 1974.

Freire, Paulo, *Pedagogy of the Oppressed*. Trans. Myra Bergman Ramos. London: Herder and Herder, 1970.

Fuller, Edmund, ed. *The Christian Idea of Education*. New Haven, Conn.: Yale University Press, 1957.

Glasser, William. *Schools Without Failure*. New York: Harper & Row, 1969.

Goodman, Paul. *Compulsory Miseducation*. New York: Penguin Books, 1971.

Guinness, Os. *The Dust of Death*. London: InterVarsity Press, 1973.

Harré, R. *The Philosophies of Science: An Introductory Study*. London: Oxford University Press, 1972.

Hill, Brian V. *Called to Teach*. Sydney, Australia: Angus & Robertson, 1971.

————. *Education and the Endangered Individual*. New York: Teachers College Press, 1973, and Dell Paperbacks, 1975.

————. *A Teenager Is Many People*. Sydney, Australia: ANZEA Press, 1971.

Hirst, P. H., and R. S. Peters. *The Logic of Education*. London: Routledge & Kegan Paul, 1972.

Hogg, Anna C. *A Christian in the Professions*. Sydney, Australia: ATCF Books, 1981.

————. *The Concept of School Discipline*. Sydney, Australia: ATCF Books, 1981.

Holt, John. *How Children Fail*. New York: Penguin Books, 1965.

Illich, Ivan. *Deschooling Society*. New York: Harper & Row, 1970.

Jeffreys, M. V. C. *Glaucon: An Inquiry into the Aims of Education*. London: Pitman, 1957.

————. *Mystery of Man*. London: Pitman, 1957.

Judges, A. V., ed. *Education and the Philosophic Mind*. London: Harrap & Co., 1957.

————. *The Function of Teaching*. London: Faber & Faber, 1959.

Kierkegaard, Sören. *A Kierkegaard Anthology*. Ed. Robert Bretall. London: Oxford University Press, 1947.

Kleinig, John. *Philosophical Issues in Education*. London: Croom Helm, 1982.

Kuhn, Thomas S. *The Structure of Scientific Revolutions*. Chicago: University of Chicago Press, 1968.

Lewis, C. S. *The Abolition of Man*. London: Geoffrey Bles, 1947.

————. *Experiment with Criticism*. Cambridge: Cambridge University Press, 1961.

Lonergan, Bernard. *Insight*. London: Longmans Green & Co., 1957.

MacKay, Donald, ed. *Christianity in a Mechanistic Universe*. London: InterVarsity Press, 1965.

Marcuse, Herbert. *One-Dimensional Man*. London: Abacus, 1972.

Maritain, Jacques. *The Education of Man*. Ed. Donald and Idella Gallagher. New York: Doubleday, 1962.

Martin, Charles. *You've Got to Start Somewhere*. London: InterVarsity Press, 1980.

Mill, John Stuart. *On Liberty*. London: J. M. Dent, 1954.

Niebuhr, Reinhold. *The Nature and Destiny of Man*. 2 vols. London: Nisbet & Co., 1943.

―――――. *The Self and the Dramas of History*. London: Faber & Faber, 1955.

Nyberg, David, ed. *The Philosophy of Open Education*. London: Routledge & Kegan Paul, 1975.

Peters, R. S. *Authority, Responsibility and Education*. 3rd ed. London: George Allen & Unwin, 1973.

―――――. *Ethics and Education*. London: George Allen & Unwin, 1966.

―――――. *Psychology and Ethical Development*. London: George Allen & Unwin, 1974.

Phenix, Philip H. *Realms of Meaning*. New York: McGraw-Hill, 1964.

Polanyi, Michael. *Personal Knowledge*. London: Routledge & Kegan Paul, 1958.

―――――. *The Tacit Dimension*. London: Routledge & Kegan Paul, 1969.

Rawls, John. *A Theory of Justice*. Cambridge, Mass: Harvard University Press, 1971.

Reimer, Everett. *School Is Dead*. New York: Penguin Books, 1971.

Rogers, Carl. *Freedom to Learn*. New York: Charles E. Merrill, 1969.

Schaeffer, Francis. *Escape from Reason*. London: InterVarsity Press, 1968.

Silberman, Melvin L., ed. *The Experience of Schooling*. New York: Holt, Rinehart & Winston, 1971.

Smart, Ninian. *Secular Education and the Logic of Religion*. London: Faber & Faber, 1968.

Snook, Ivan, ed. *Concepts of Indoctrination*. London: Routledge & Kegan Paul, 1972.

Stedman, Ray C. *Body Life*. 2nd ed. Glendale, Calif.: Regal Publications, 1977.

Trigg, Roger. *Reason and Commitment*. Cambridge: Cambridge University Press, 1973.

Wardle, David. *The Rise of the Schooled Society*. London: Routledge & Kegan Paul, 1974.

White, John. *The Cost of Commitment*. London: InterVarsity Press, 1977.

White, John P. *Towards a Compulsory Curriculum*. London: Routledge & Kegan Paul, 1973.

Index of Subjects

Index of Names